SPIRIT
TALKER

SPIRIT TALKER

INDIGENOUS STORIES AND TEACHINGS
FROM A MI'KMAQ PSYCHIC MEDIUM

SHAWN LEONARD

HAY HOUSE, INC.
Carlsbad, California • New York City
London • Sydney • New Delhi

Copyright © 2023 by Shawn Leonard

Published in the United States by: Hay House, Inc.: www.hayhouse.com®
• *Published in Australia by:* Hay House Australia Pty. Ltd.: www.hayhouse
.com.au • *Published in the United Kingdom by:* Hay House UK, Ltd.:
www.hayhouse.co.uk • *Published in India by:* Hay House Publishers
India: www.hayhouse.co.in

Cover design: Scott Breidenthal
Interior design: Karim Garcia
Interior illustrations: Darryl LeBlanc

Cataloging-in-Publication Data is on file at the Library of Congress

Tradepaper ISBN: 978-1-4019-7123-6
E-book ISBN: 978-1-4019-7124-3
Audiobook ISBN: 978-1-4019-7125-0

12 11 10 9 8 7 6 5 4 3
1st edition, August 2023

Printed in the United States of America

This product uses papers sourced from responsibly managed forests. For
more information, see www.hayhouse.com.

*This book is dedicated to every person
I have connected to throughout my journey,
as every single one has helped me become
the person I am. To my father, James, for
the ultimate sacrifice of leaving this world
to show me the light. To my Spirit guides,
Sam and Victoria, my Ancestors,
and all my Spirit tribe.*

*Thank you to all the Elders and all the
Indigenous cultures I have encountered that
have shared their light and knowledge with me.*

*I especially dedicate this book to every spirit
who has entrusted me with their messages.*

*Wela'lioq—Msit No'kmaq.
Thank you all—We are all related.*

CONTENTS

FOREWORD

As a medicine woman, best-selling author, and spiritual entrepreneur, I have worked with thousands of folks who are searching to connect to a deeper part of themselves. Indigenous ways of knowing and being are what bring them into my sacred space, and they find reconnection and remembering in our time together. My spirit name, Healing Rainbow Woman, shares the essence of my soul work: a bridge that invites humanity to come together with compassion. At this time on the earth, folks are desiring reconnection and a return home to self. My medicine helps folks to bridge the earth and spirit realms, wisdom that my Ancestors have held since time immemorial.

As Indigenous people, there has been so much trauma that has disconnected us from our spirituality and the teachings of the land. Colonialism attempted to strip us of this most sacred connection. Our relationship to Earth, creation, and the spirit world was deemed primitive or unholy. So much was broken and there was so much separation of our innate ways of being. Therefore, it's brave and often challenging work to reclaim, remember, and share the medicines that flow through our bones and blood.

Sharing our gifts with the world is a powerful journey when we carry generational harm in our blood. It is not a journey for the fainthearted, for one must intentionally choose to walk with the Seven Sacred Grandfather teachings of truth, love, bravery, humility, honesty, wisdom, and respect. Shawn Leonard is one of these people who has chosen this path, the path that in my Anishinaabe teachings is called mino-bimaadiziwin—the one who walks in a good way.

Years ago, I remember seeing advertisements for the show *Spirit Talker* on APTN, an Indigenous station in Canada. I was in awe as I watched this humble yet potent Indigenous man sharing his medicine with the world, visibly and courageously. It was rare to see Indigenous people sharing their gifts in this way. Beading, drumming, dancing—yes. Indigenous mediumship, not so much. I felt excited, knowing that even though we are from different nations, there was someone from the same culture, who was sharing his spirit-led work.

I remember feeling a deep resonance with his path, as he, too, was one who lived between worlds. Witnessing Shawn accurately and precisely accessing the realms beyond this earthly existence was inspiring and exciting. I began following his journey and cheered him on from the sidelines. I wholeheartedly believe that when one Indigenous voice makes an impact, it helps to raise all our voices. Shawn has been that trailblazer for me, an Indigenous visionary who continues to pave the way.

Spirit Talker: Indigenous Stories and Teachings from a Mi'kmaq Psychic Medium is a brilliant account of Shawn Leonard's medicine walk. True to our traditional ways of passing down wisdom, this book is filled with vibrant and profound storytelling that honors all the experiences, people, and spirit connections that have lined his path. This book is an invitation to contemplate the divine essence that we were in spirit form before we entered our physical bodies. It is the same form that we will return to when we leave this earth. Furthermore, the real-life stories give credence to the thin veil that exists between worlds.

As I read the pages, I found myself in constant wonder, as the words reminded me of the eternal existence of our spiritual energy. The stories often brought tears of joy and compassion, and you can feel the enormous heart-medicine that Shawn holds for all of humanity.

As a spirit talker, Shawn has been blessed with the ability to understand another language, the language of Spirit. This book invites the reader to contemplate their connection to divine creation energy. This is a powerful contemplation when the outside world attempts to sway us from our true nature. In sitting and learning with Elders and other traditional teachers, Shawn is a wisdom keeper in his own right, sharing Indigenous medicine ways to offer balance and help us all live in the right relationship with the earth and one another.

This book will help to heal broken hearts and offer hope to many. In a world that has been divided, *Spirit Talker* weaves much-needed light into our awareness, hearts, and minds. For those feeling disconnected from their purpose or presence in this world, Shawn's stories will help you see that you matter. As you move through *Spirit Talker*, each chapter offers an opportunity to trust in a reality that moves beyond our earthbound, physical existence. The words of this book remind us that we are energy in motion and that death is not the end. Our eternal light shines on.

As an Indigenous medium, Shawn's voice is a fresh and powerful addition to the world of spiritual teachers and guides. I am deeply grateful for his example of leadership, vision, and visibility. With every step he takes, he blesses the planet with good medicine, walking with mino-bimaadiziwin. This book is a must-read and it is my hope that you come away from it remembering your sacred place in creation.

Chi miigwetch (Thank you,)

Asha Frost
Nenaandawi Nagweyab Kwe
Healing Rainbow Woman, Crane Clan
Best-selling author of *You Are the Medicine*

INTRODUCTION

Kwe', welta'si na' pekisin ("Hello, I'm glad you came," in Mi'kmaq).

Through this incredible gift of life, we all have a purpose and a calling deep within our souls: to be the best we can and to learn unconditional love for ourselves and for others. It is through this love my calling and life's purpose became known.

The wisdom and insight I have gained from my experiences have been nothing short of life changing. In fact, the trajectory of my time on this physical earth has become so clear that it has changed every aspect of how I see reality. It made me realize how we are all connected—even after supposed death—to the point I no longer believe in death. Death is an illusion.

We all have been taught, in the scientific method, that energy cannot be destroyed, but instead it transforms into something else or transfers to somewhere else. Into what or where, however, cannot be explained with the same method—even with modern science. We do not cease to live when we leave this physical life; rather, we transform into our true essence (that of the spirit) and return to our true home within the light.

Looking back, I can see how every experience brought me to the knowledge and understanding I have today. In this book I share some of these remarkable experiences, which are taken from real life and real people alive in both the physical and spiritual worlds. If I had not lived to experience them myself, I am not sure I would truly believe.

It is through the process of spirit communication that I was taught a new language: the language of Spirit. It is a universal language that transcends all spoken languages, on this planet and every planet in the universe.

I never took a class in this language; I never took a course on spirituality. Rather, it is something that just revealed itself to me; and I feel as though this was my true calling all my life—made, perhaps, as a soul contract before my current incarnation as Shawn Leonard. Perhaps I was chosen in this way to help people come to a new understanding of the spiritual world.

I have trouble calling this knowledge and understanding a gift, as so many people refer to it. I like to tell people I know another language, and that I am a spirit talker. I truly feel blessed to have had these experiences, which have helped form my ever-changing reality.

Through my life's journey I have learned about the spirit world, spirit communication, spirit guides, angels, animal totems, and reincarnation. Most rewarding of all, I have rediscovered my lost Indigenous culture and how spiritually enriched our culture is.

Indigenous people have always had an incredible blend of life and Spirit. It has been taken from us, and now is the time for us to remember and help the balance return to our world. We are all living in the same sacred hoop of life.

My intention with writing and sharing these experiences is to help you see the world as I do, as not everybody has the same insight into the spiritual realm. Every day, through my culture, my readings, my live events, and my encounters with the spirit world, I continue to learn.

In sharing my story, wisdom, and knowledge, I hope it will help you change how you see the physical and spiritual worlds. Shifting your perspective in such a way will allow you to encounter these great gifts in your own life; you will encounter the spirit world with new eyes. You will have the wisdom, and vision, to know our Creator resides in us all. You will gain the ability to see, feel, hear, and know the spirit within yourself, and help return balance of life and Spirit once again.

I firmly believe we are made of the visible and invisible universe, with the Great Spirit as our Creator. Almost 99 percent of the mass of the human body is comprised of six elements: oxygen, carbon, hydrogen, nitrogen, calcium, and phosphorus. If you break down every particle, there isn't anything solid—just energy vibrating at your ever-changing frequency.

This means that at every moment we become a new creation on a cellular level. In the same way, we become a new creation on a spiritual level with every new experience. Yet we all exist in this world as conscious, living human beings. We couldn't have consciousness if it wasn't abundant in the universe, and if we were not all part of, and made from, it.

You were surrounded by our Creator's loving energy before your conceived incarnation in what you perceive as your present earthly form. Spirit is your true form, meaning you have never been separated from our Creator, nor the greater consciousness of all spirits.

Each and every single person on this earth is equally important, and as we evolve our Creator evolves alongside us through our experiences—through this life and every life we live. The experience of our Creator extends to everything in our world and to every planet in the universe.

We cannot be separated from that which resides within, or from that which is all around us. It is the bond of love from our Creator that binds us all. When we love our family, our friends, our pets, our planet, when we admire the vastness and greatness of the universe, we are loving and honoring our Creator. We are all one.

Even if you feel separate from the people or animals you loved who are now within the spirit world, remember this is also an illusion. Allow me to help you understand how they are still with you, and how they still communicate with you. I am glad the Great Spirit, our Creator, found a way to guide you to my book. I pray my experiences, my story, and my knowledge enlighten you and give you a new understanding of both the spirit world and spirit communication.

I ultimately hope my stories help you to remember who you are, and that you walk with balance in the sacred hoop of life, knowing you have a divine purpose, and you are, and always have been, Spirit.

Wela'lin (Thank you)
Enjoy, and share in my wisdom with love.

CHAPTER 1

JIJAQMIJE'L TA'N TELITPIAQEWE'L

EARLY SPIRITUAL EXPERIENCES

To an outsider, my early life may have appeared perfectly "normal," yet my childhood was filled with extraordinary experiences. These amazing events paved the way to who I am now—what I call a spirit talker and what others call a medium. I consider this life to be my destiny. I'm forever grateful to my mother who, although a devout Catholic, had a strong belief in the afterlife and Spirit's ability to communicate with those still living. When I was five, my great-grandparents, both recently deceased, appeared in my room late one night to talk to me. My mother assured me this was normal and people who had just died often drop by and visit. When she heard my imaginary friend, Sam, had some controversial things to say, she merely said, "Well, Sam and I don't agree." When she found out I could leave my body at night and fly around the neighborhood, her response was "Just make sure you come back in the morning!"

Sam was another spiritual figure from my childhood, one who never frightened me and who I never wanted to send away. He was what adults often refer to as an imaginary friend. Except Sam wasn't imaginary! Up to the time I was five he was my constant companion, joining me as I played. Sam was probably in his late 20s or early 30s, about six feet tall with dirty-blond hair and piercing blue eyes. Although he seemed very "flesh and blood" to me, Sam was one of my spirit guides. In fact, he still is.

Sam was someone I could see, hear, and even feel. He used to grab my hand and sometimes playfully shove me. He was as real to me as any other living person, so when he completely disappeared it was quite traumatic. The day he left was an ordinary day. I was down in the basement, playing with my Dinky cars. Sam was with me, like he always was, but I remember him telling me he had to go. "Shawn," he said, "I have to leave, but I want you to know I'm always going to be with you, even though you won't be able to see me anymore. If you ever need me, just talk to me."

There was a big flash of the whitest light I had ever seen—and he was gone. Sam had completely vanished.

I suddenly felt so alone in a way I never had up to that point, and in a way that felt completely wrong. I remember crying and crying all day. I tried to talk to my friend but wasn't able to see or hear him anymore. It was devastating.

A couple of years later I again had a direct experience with Sam. It was not in a physical form this time, but in a way that made me understand he really was still with me like he had promised. I was just learning to ride a bike and was being reckless, setting up ramps on steep hills. As I was barreling down one such hill, I hit the ramp the wrong way and went flying. But while in the air, I suddenly felt my body being grabbed and turned upright, so instead of landing on my head I landed on my feet, and I wasn't injured at all. The other kids were in awe, as was I. To them it looked like a miracle, but I knew it was Sam.

Although my spirit guide no longer appeared in physical form past the time I was five, there were other magical things I was able to hold on to a little longer. The ability to leave my body at night and fly through my town was one of them. We've all had dreams of flying, but this was different. For one thing, it happened like clockwork every night, in that strange state between being awake and being asleep. For another, my town looked ever so slightly different. There was always a dusky half-light I have come to think of as the light of the astral world, which is closely layered on top of our own, and to which, as a child, I had direct access.

Every night it was the same thing. I would be falling asleep when I'd suddenly find myself standing in front of my house. I'd then make up my mind as to which direction I wanted to go, and then off I'd fly, zipping through the sky. The topography was the same, and so was the placement of all the houses. The only thing different was that there were never any people in this dusk world. Never, that is, but for one exception.

On that occasion I saw an older woman, wearing a long, dark Victorian-style dress, floating over the telephone poles. She had an umbrella like Mary Poppins and looked as though she was straight out of the 1800s. When I tried to talk to her, she just looked at me, stuck up her nose, and floated on by. Excited by her presence, there was another person whom I looked for in this dusk world, yet never found. His name was David, and he was a classmate who died of leukemia when I was about six years old. When he passed, I told my mom I was going to use my nighttime flights to find him. That evening I flew to his house, but no one was there. When I awoke the next morning, I told my mom I hadn't been able to find him, and she assured me this was because he was now in heaven. These two experiences—seeing the woman dressed in period clothing and being unable to find David—helped form my beliefs about the astral world.

I believe it is a place of lower vibration, where spirits who haven't fully embraced the light still reside. It is a place that exists between our realities here on Earth and those in the spirit world. I had these nighttime adventures until I was about eight or nine years old and can clearly remember realizing my ability to fly was leaving me. I would fall asleep and still appear outside my house, but I would remain earthbound.

Little did I know that my nighttime flights, visits from my great-grandparents, and my conversations with Sam were just a taste of what was to come. But first, in order to remember, I had to forget.

CHAPTER 2

KEJITPAQTEK AQ WESOQWEK

THE DARK AND THE LIGHT

And forget I did.

By the time I was 15, anything not connected to the reality of my daily life was ancient history. Brushes with the spirit world had been replaced by crushes on girls, practicing the guitar, and starting to learn things about being an adult. My dad was one of my biggest teachers in this respect.

With 22 years of military service behind him, my dad was due to retire in only three years. He told me he was sick of traveling and being away from his family for such long periods. His plan was to continue to work to bring in money, while still having his pension supplement our family's income.

In the fall of 1987, my dad was building a garage so he could tinker with his vehicles outside during the winter. On October 14, we had just finished framing the structure and were waiting for the cement to be poured. We were taking a break in the kitchen, having a glass of water, when I noticed how much my dad was sweating. I chalked it up to hard work, but then he told me he had a really bad cramp in his left hand and wondered aloud if he should be worried.

Then, two days later, I woke up to my mom yelling for help. "There's something wrong with your dad. He's out in the driveway. His truck is running but I can't wake him up."

In an emergency, time does funny things. The few short minutes during which I tried to resuscitate my father seemed to pass very slowly. Questioning whether I had the number of chest compressions correct, I attempted to breathe life back into him, to no avail. I remember screaming at him, telling his spirit to get back into his body and return to us. I also pled with the Creator. Suddenly, there were neighbors present and I was walking into the house to tell my mom that Dad wasn't coming back.

He was only 42. I don't remember much about the days that followed. I did not want what happened to be true, and I found it very hard to focus. In fact, I failed ninth grade that year because although I would go to school, I wasn't really present. Needless to say, it was a very tough time.

Over the next year, I did the same things other 16-year-olds do: listened to loud music, grew my hair long, joined a band, smoked some weed, and stayed out too late. My mother would get mad at me for not coming home on time and sneaking in and out of the house. One October night, almost a year after my dad had passed, I was out late. Not wanting to wake my mother up, I decided to sleep in the basement. Soon after I fell asleep, I woke up, only to find myself outside my body, looking down at myself sleeping on the couch. It was a similar feeling to my childhood flying dreams, in that I was hyperalert and very aware something unusual was happening.

Suddenly, an enormous white light appeared in the middle of the room. It was the largest, brightest light I had ever seen, and reminded me of the white flash when Sam disappeared from my life. But this light was even brighter and larger, and it lasted for longer than an instant. This light stayed. Then, to my great surprise and delight, my father walked out of it.

He looked fantastic: incredibly healthy and smiling broadly, but without his trademark eyeglasses. He was wearing a white robe. My father emanated tremendous love and joy as he looked at me, and the word "glistening" came to my mind as I smiled back. He was just so vibrant.

"Oh my God, Dad!" The moment the words were out of my mouth I went quickly from elation to anger, asking why the hell he'd left us. I told him how bad things had been since he died, how Mom was struggling to pay off the mortgage. "I hardly saw you because you were gone all the time, and then you had to die? It's not fair."

My dad just smiled and told me to calm down. "I have some things to tell you, Shawn. There are a few things you need to know," he said. "The first thing is that I'm okay and I'm in a good place. You need to tell your mom and your brother that I love them and I'm watching over them."

He continued talking and, as he did, I looked behind him into the light. I could see ornate, white marble pillars. "You're not going to understand this right now," he said, "but everything happens for a reason. This was my time to leave, and that was the plan before you or I were even born. It was my time to go home."

As if that weren't enough information, he went on. "I want you to remember this light; this light is everything. You're going to help people know this, and you're going to help them understand why we're here and where we go after we die."

This bit of information stopped me in my tracks. "What are you talking about?" I asked.

"I know this doesn't make sense now, but it will," he said. I was completely bewildered. "What do you mean I'm going to help people? How the hell am I supposed to do that?" He smiled at me, full of love. "Don't worry. When the time comes, Shawn, you won't have to do anything! It'll just be something that happens. You'll know what I mean when it does."

As we spoke, I became rather entranced by the world behind my father, the one from which he had so suddenly appeared. I was mostly fixated on the alluring, magnificent light, and the way it felt. There was something about it that felt like home, and I found myself wanting to see more of the world where my father now was; I wanted to experience the feeling of walking into that light.

As if reading my mind, my father suddenly turned serious. "Shawn, you can look, but I can't let you come here."

"Why not?" I asked. "I promise I'll come right back."

He then informed me that if I walked into the light I would want to stay. As he was saying this, I strongly felt the so-called realness of the place waiting behind my father. This is hard to explain, because to most of us our world feels so real and solid, but as I looked and compared the two it was as if our world paled and shrunk in comparison to what lay beyond. I wanted so badly to experience it for myself. I even tried to sneak past him, but he intercepted me with a light touch to the middle of my forehead and said, "Shawn, just remember what I have said." I was suddenly back in my body, on the couch. I lay there for a long time, looking at the space where he had appeared, willing both my father and the light to return.

But they never did.

CHAPTER 3

PILEY POQTAMKIAQ
A NEW BEGINNING

It was incredibly soothing to see my father again, especially to see him looking so well and happy. The experience stayed with me. The part about my dad telling me I would help people was mystifying, however, and I soon forgot. It just didn't make sense. Simply knowing my dad still loved me and watched over me somehow secured me to my life again. It was then things began to shift.

I made a couple of new friends who weren't as into smoking marijuana as the rest of the high school crowd. I started playing guitar, in earnest this time. I also started dating someone, and for the first time in my life I felt as though I'd fallen in love.

My grades improved and my friends and I graduated. Suddenly, we all needed to decide what we were doing with our lives. As someone who enjoyed being outside and doing physical labor, working at the lumber mill seemed the best option.

It was backbreaking work, and the guys I worked with were a bit rough. I lasted one month; just long enough for me to do the math and figure out that the most money I would ever make at the lumber mill was about $14 an hour.

Enter my Newfoundland grandmother. She told me my Uncle Sam was looking for a fishing partner. Having loved spending summers with this part of my family I was quick to say yes, and I spent the next year living the life of a fisherman. That year I also spent a lot of time with my grandmother. One of the things I grew up knowing, but didn't think about a lot, was the fact my grandmother had grown up in the Native community of Miawpukek— Conne River. She is Mi'kmaq but left her community to marry my grandfather. Sometimes we would visit the place she grew up, but for the most part our Mi'kmaq heritage wasn't something we really acknowledged nor talked about.

During my time in Newfoundland, all of that changed. My grandmother and I would stay up playing cards. She would weave in stories of her family and the years growing up, smoking the whole time she spoke. Her grandmother had been a medicine woman, so she was privy to all kinds of healing remedies.

One of the most important, and surprising, things I learned about my grandmother was that she could see and feel and hear things other people couldn't. It wasn't unusual for her to be washing the dishes at the kitchen sink, only to suddenly grab the broom and run outside. I would watch her chase something through the yard, something I couldn't see, while yelling and brandishing the broom. She would return, out of breath, yet triumphant.

"There was a bad spirit out there," she would say. "I chased it away!" I know now we share the same gift: that of being in touch with Spirit.

After some time, I was contacted by mom's youngest sister, who lived in Calgary, Alberta. She was dating a guy who worked for an office furniture company. It was growing fast, and they needed some new workers. I weighed my options: stay in Nova Scotia and work at the lumber mill or go back to Newfoundland. Or try something completely different.

I opted for different. Calgary seemed a big, exciting city, and I was more than ready for something new. I packed a bag and bought a one-way ticket. I had a place to stay, $200 in my wallet, and the prospect of work on the horizon.

I took a deep breath, said good-bye to Nova Scotia, and flew off into a whole new chapter of my life. One that would open a door to my future self; the self I was surprised to find waiting for me.

CHAPTER 4

WE'JITU'N IKNMAQNM

DISCOVERING THE GIFT

Only a week into my new life in Calgary, I had a job at the office furniture company in the metal fabrication department. Shortly thereafter, I went to a Canada Day concert with a few friends and met the woman I would end up marrying—Marissa. Real life was happening quickly now.

After two years of dating, Marissa got pregnant, and we decided to get married before the baby was born. I quickly moved into a permanent position within the company, building custom office furniture. I enjoyed it, and felt as though I'd finally found my niche.

When I think about what happened next, I marvel at how the Great Spirit waited until my life had settled and I had achieved some stability before it pulled out all the stops and really started to show me my soul's purpose. And it started at a coffee shop, of all places.

I had a friend named Jimmy, who worked at a coffee shop, and after picking up the baby from the sitter I'd go and meet him after work. While we worked, the coffee shop's hustle and bustle all around us, I would start to recognize the faces of the people he worked with every day. Slowly, I realized I would get a feeling, a sort of knowing, about certain people. There was one guy who I thought was stealing from the till. I never saw anything odd, it was just a feeling I had. I felt the same with another guy I suspected was dealing drugs. I shared these feelings with Jimmy.

To my surprise, within a one-week period I had heard from Jimmy that the first guy got caught stealing and was fired. The second guy got arrested and thrown in jail for dealing drugs. I remember Jimmy coming to my home and telling me what had happened, asking incredulously, "How did you know that?"

I told him what I thought was true: that it was just a vibe I picked up on and that everyone could do it. Jimmy didn't agree. He thought it was something more and confided in a few of his friends about what happened. One of his friends, a self-confessed psychic junkie named Amber, heard the story and asked Jimmy if I could "read" her. I didn't really know what that meant.

The whole idea made me nervous. I had no idea what I would say or what "reading" someone entailed. I didn't know what I was doing! My friend reassured me, saying I should just tell Amber whatever popped into my head.

The night arrived and Amber came over to my house. I was still nervous, but after what had happened at the restaurant, I was also curious as to what I could (if anything) pick up from someone I didn't know. This was a living experiment, right in front of me on the couch. I didn't know a thing about Amber except that she worked with Jimmy. So, I just went with it.

"I think you're going to meet a guy named Don, and it's a romantic thing. You'll be interested in each other."

"I just met a guy named Don."

Being a so-called psychic junkie, Amber didn't look as surprised as I felt. *I can't believe I got a name right*, I thought to myself. *How did I do that?* I went on. "I have a feeling you're a writer, and you're going to write a book."

"Well, I am working on a book."

My stomach was doing flip-flops. Was this real? Or was I just really good at guessing? Amber was excited, and so was I. She then cut right to the chase.

"Can you connect with someone in the spirit world?" She was sitting on the edge of the couch now, staring at me intently.

"What?" I wasn't sure I'd heard her correctly. "Someone in the spirit world. Someone who died."

I had heard her right. "I don't think so. I don't know. I've never done that before."

"Can you try? There's someone who I've always wanted to connect with."

It seemed so important. I didn't want to disappoint. I stared at the wall behind the couch and my logical brain kicked in. I tried to focus by concentrating on the fact she wanted a message from her grandmother—or someone like that. But what came surprised me. I saw a teenaged boy, standing in what looked like a suburban backyard, dressed in a baseball uniform. He was looking at me while tossing a ball up and down in one hand. He did that for a while, then turned and walked into the shed behind him. I had no idea why this image popped into my mind, and I was positive it wasn't what she was looking for.

I won't ever forget the look on Amber's face when I told her, or the tears that immediately began rolling down her cheeks. "That's him," she said. "He was my best friend and we played baseball together. He was battling depression, and one night after a game he went out to his shed and took his own life."

Oh my God.

Amber continued, "I've always wanted to know if he was okay. Do you think he's alright now?"

I was trying to hide my own shock about what had just happened, while also rapidly trying to process and understand it. My first thought was, *I must be a mind reader.* I must have simply read her thoughts. She was thinking about him and, somehow, I picked that up.

Amber interrupted my inner turmoil. "Shawn, is he okay? Is he happy?"

I didn't know! But I sensed how important this was to her. "This is all new to me. I really don't know how he is now, but I'm sure he's okay."

When Amber left my house that night, she was really happy. So happy, in fact, she went to work and told all her co-workers. Then she went out with her friends and told all of them. She told her family too. I started getting phone calls. People wanted to set up a time to meet with me; people who wanted me to "read" them, and others who wanted to connect with loved ones who had died.

In the days after my time with Amber my mind was reeling and shut doors all over the place. There was no way dead people were communicating with me. No way! It was too out there. It couldn't be. But it was.

CHAPTER 5

WELIWSUA'TMK JIJAQMIJ AKNUTMASK

EMBRACING SPIRIT COMMUNICATION

From nine to five, every day, my life looked just as it used to. Yet in my downtime, after work and on weekends, things were suddenly very different and very interesting. I received so much interest in my readings that a few weeks after my first reading with Amber, I was already booked solid for three months. I certainly hadn't yet embraced it fully, but there was no doubt people were getting something out of the readings.

All the while, I kept asking myself how this was happening. I had never taken a class, nor had any training, and I didn't know much about spiritual things. Was I a mind reader? Was I able to pick up on people's thoughts and their memories of those who had passed on? Is that what this gift was?

I kept expecting I would wake up, that my life would return to the way it used to be. But that didn't happen. This was real. As that slowly dawned upon me—that this thing I never expected was now a big part of my life—I decided to be as open as possible and learn as much as I could.

It was a rich time with a lot of new experiences flooding in, some of which took some time getting used to. At night, just before drifting off to sleep, I began to see faces. These weren't faces of people I knew. Rather, it was like a Rolodex of random faces, flashing one after the other in quick succession. A wide variety of faces, looking right at me, in a constant flow. I couldn't get to sleep each night without first seeing what felt like a thousand faces.

During the day, I felt as though my intuition was increasingly spot on. I would have flashes of insight, instances of just knowing something, only to then have it confirmed. This knowing bled into my work life. I was coming around to the idea that I was a mind reader, someone who could tune into people's energy if they were in the vicinity. Then something happened to radically shift that idea.

One of my longtime co-workers was a man named Orhan. We had become friends, so during this period of my life, I would confide in Orhan the new abilities I seemed to have acquired. One day, while at our desks, I heard a name in my head, as if on repeat. The name was Charlie. It felt like a voice separate from my own, as if someone was whispering to me through my mind, and the experience continued for nearly an hour.

I turned to Orhan, and suddenly the voice stopped. I looked away, back at my computer, when it started again. I looked back at Orhan and it stopped. I was still freaked out, but now a little relieved. *This must be the mind reader thing*, I thought. *Orhan must be thinking about a friend named Charlie, and that's what I'm picking up.*

I had to know, however, and braced myself for Orhan's disbelief. "Orhan, I have to ask you something. Do you know a guy named Charlie?"

Slowly, Orhan turned toward me. "Why do you ask that?"

There was something about the way he spoke that sent a quick chill down my spine. I didn't know what nerve I'd hit, but I had definitely hit one. "The name Charlie just keeps popping in my head," I said. "You must be thinking about him?"

"I'm not thinking about him right now. But I was thinking about him a couple of weeks ago. He's someone I used to work with at the airport, around eight years ago."

As soon as Orhan said that, I got an image of a sign for a local bar in Calgary. It was called the T&C, for Town and Country. "Why am I seeing the sign for the T&C now?" I said this mostly to myself, but Orhan overheard.

"What did you say?" he asked, but this time his whole body tensed, and his eyes locked onto mine. "I'm pretty sure that was the last place Charlie was seen alive."

It was as if all the air had suddenly been sucked out of my lungs, and I shivered with intense goose bumps. *Does that mean he's now dead?* Why would I be getting an image of the last place this Charlie—whom I didn't even know—was last seen?

"Is he dead? Is Charlie dead?"

"Yeah. He was murdered." Orhan narrowed his eyes.

Just then another image came. It felt as though I were standing at the top of a set of stairs and there were people all around me, and then I was walking down the stairs. Down the stairs, over and over. "And now I'm seeing stairs, someone going down a flight of stairs." I was so shocked by these sudden and vivid images I couldn't help speaking them out loud. "And you're not thinking any of these things I am seeing?" I was completely bewildered.

"No! I wasn't thinking about Charlie or the Town and Country or stairs. I don't know what you're talking about." Orhan stopped. "Have you been talking to someone I used to work with?" he whispered.

I was still reeling from the last image, and it took a moment to realize Orhan was accusing me of being some sort of con artist. "I haven't talked to anyone. I didn't even know you worked at the airport, so how could I know who you worked with?"

"I don't know what you're doing, but I don't like this at all. Just stop it." Orhan turned his whole body around and faced his computer.

My mind was in overdrive, trying to process what was happening. *If Orhan wasn't just thinking about Charlie, how did Charlie's name come into my head?* This was entirely new territory. I felt as though I were desperately trying to shove all the puzzle pieces into place, but nothing fit. In the meantime, my friend was now mad at me and thought I was messing with his head. He was frustrated with me, so I decided to drop it.

One day, about two months after the strange conversation with Orhan, I left the gym and headed to work. I stopped for a coffee, and finding I had a little extra time, I did something I usually didn't have the chance to do in those days: I picked up a newspaper.

When I got to the office, I still had 10 minutes before I had to work, so I sat down with my coffee and the *Calgary Sun* and started flipping. Right away, an article about an unsolved murder caught my attention. A former airport employee named Manequin Achari, who went by the nickname Charlie, had been found dead in his basement apartment eight years prior. He was last seen at the Town and Country, and his killer was still at large. The police were still looking for information that might lead to an arrest.

I felt as though I'd been hit by a ton of bricks. When Orhan walked in a few minutes later, I shoved the newspaper at him. "Orhan, you need to read this!" He took it, read it, and turned to me. "Do you remember us talking about your friend Charlie?" I asked him.

He sighed. "What do you want me to say?"

"I want you to tell me you remember the part where I said the thing about the stairs. They found his body in a basement apartment! Did you know anything about him living in a basement apartment?"

"That's right. I didn't know. Why is that so important?"

"Because if you didn't know about him living in a basement apartment, then you weren't thinking about stairs, which means I am not a mind reader, and that the information came from some other source." Orhan looked dubious.

"Orhan, I really, really need you to be honest with me, and I need you to swear you're telling me the truth. Are you sure you don't know anything about where or how this guy died?" Orhan swore it.

Everything changed in that moment. If I hadn't picked up all that information from Orhan, then where was it coming from? Was it possible it was coming from Charlie?

Was it possible I was receiving communications from the spirit world?

This idea suddenly felt very real and very alive to me. In the same moment, I remembered my father's visit and what he had said to me: that I would be helping people understand why we are here, and where we go after we die. He told me I didn't have to do anything. That it would just happen. He was right.

CHAPTER 6

TAWE AQ M'SNT+SK

ASK AND YOU
SHALL RECEIVE

After that experience, the floodgates opened. It was as though I had suddenly given myself permission to remember every mystical or otherworldly experience I had ever had, but couldn't make sense of at the time.

I realized the spirit world had important and life-changing things to say to the people who were my clients. It was very humbling to know there were spirits on the other side using me as a conduit to connect with their loved ones. When people cried tears of relief or joy in my living room during a reading because of something I had seen, I often remembered what my father had said about helping others. Every day was exciting and new. I couldn't wait to talk to people; I couldn't wait to see what I could envision next. It was—and still is—a learning experience to see what new information would come into my mind and how it would make itself known.

Another shift came when I started doing readings over the phone. It was something I had been reluctant to try, even though I knew other mediums and psychics read people this way. I wasn't sure if the energy would be the same, but I was getting a lot of messages to trust myself. As it turned out, there was absolutely no difference in what I was able to pick up in person. I knew I was on the right track, and when I allowed myself to feel this way there was a sense of destiny; it was building inside me and strongly pulling me forward.

The only problem was there are only so many hours in a week, and at least 40 of those went to my full-time job. I thought about becoming a medium full time, but I and Marissa feared losing financial stability. There was no guarantee I would continue to stay busy as a medium, and even though I strongly felt this was my calling I wasn't yet confident enough to make the leap. None of this stopped me from continuing to build communication with the spirit world. At the time, I was meditating and praying daily—taking time to connect with my spirit guides as well as the spirit of my father. I used to ask him for signs that he was with me and began to see three things consistently: blue jays, feathers, and dimes. To me, the dimes were a perfect representation of my father. The coin is worth 10 cents, and my father died in the 10th month of the year. Dimes are imprinted with the image of a sailing ship on one side, which matches with the fact that my father was a sailor. Often, the dimes I found would have the year 1987 on them—the year my dad died. My father sent me so many dimes, in fact, that I started joking with him. "Dad, if you're gonna send me dimes could you send me something a little bigger? What about coins worth more, or dollar bills?" Apparently, all I had to do was ask because that's exactly what started to happen.

It began with loonies, the Canadian one-dollar coin. The first one I found was buried in the ice of a 7-Eleven parking lot, but when I dug it out, I discovered the year imprinted on it was 1987. I knew then he had heard me, and it made me wonder how much more was possible. I started to specifically ask for larger bills, and fives and tens started showing up. I remember one particular walk where the wind blew a handful of five-dollar bills at me as I was walking down the road: four of them! They blew right toward me on the breeze. The best part was a stranger helped grab them, and then handed them over like they were mine! After the twenty-dollar bills started coming I upped the ante and asked my dad for a fifty. I remember the day I found it: I was walking in the snow when I saw something pink glistening under all the white. *Is this my fifty?* I thought as I bent down and brushed the snow away. It was! I truly believe when we ask the spirit world for concrete things they are overjoyed to show us how they can make things happen. I also believe they are happy to show they can communicate in ways that are meaningful to us here on Earth. The spirit world, our angels and guides, want to help us and want to be actively involved in our lives. We just need to ask and then let them do their work.

Whether it's through somebody showing up on your doorstep or having a blue jay feather or a dime cross your path, the spirit world hears you and delights in responding to your requests. You are guided and loved every step of the way.

ASKING FOR A SIGN

The guidance I give everyone to help them see a special and unique sign from Spirit is to speak lovingly, clearly, and out loud to your loved one in the spirit world.

If you need help from your spirit guides, do the same. Even if you do not know who your guides are, talk to them out loud with all your heart.

For example: My guides, please hear my request. I wish for you to send me the perfect person to help me with this particular problem I am having, and to do it in such a way that I know you have sent them to me. Or: Mom, Dad, brother, sister, cousin (or whoever you want to contact) in the spirit world, please hear my request. I would like to receive a special and unique sign from you.

You can ask for a feather or dime or perhaps a butterfly, dragonfly, ladybug, bumblebee, or specific bird. Whatever sign you choose, ask your loved one to send it to you in such a way that it will be undeniable and absolutely obvious. I would not put a time frame on this, as the spirit world needs time to manifest this for you in an incredible way.

Enjoy this little exercise and be prepared to be amazed and know that you, too, are still guided and loved from the spirit world.

CHAPTER 7

KWILAQ N'JIJAQMIJ

SEARCHING FOR MY SPIRIT

By day, I was an employee at an office furniture company and by night, a psychic medium. Although more and more people knew about my "other" work, I wasn't part of a community of like-minded souls. After a while it started to feel like something was missing.

One day, just flipping channels on the TV, I saw the world-renowned psychic Sylvia Browne. Watching another psychic in action was a novel concept, and I was intrigued. I sought out her books and paid attention when she was a guest on talk shows. The more I learned about her, the more I sensed she was authentic. I found out she had founded a church in California called the Society of

Novus Spiritus. It was based on gnostic principles, such as the duality of God as both masculine and feminine, a belief in reincarnation, and a conviction that humans are able to directly communicate with the Divine and learn important things about their own souls' journey. There had been so much I disliked about traditional religion growing up, so these concepts were like a breath of fresh air and appealed to me right away. As I learned more about gnosticism, I felt it resonating in a very deep place within. As my research continued, I discovered there weren't any Canadian chapters of Novus Spiritus. Although there were a few study groups, none were in the Calgary area. My wife had also become interested in gnostic concepts and Browne's church, and together we decided to form a study group. It gained popularity pretty quickly, especially among the people who came to me for readings. The idea to start our own Novus Spiritus Church in Calgary gained momentum, and we decided to approach Browne's organization and ask if they'd be open to a Canadian chapter. To our delight, they liked the idea. They also agreed to send their head minister to Calgary to run a minister-in-training program.

Prior to this, it had never occurred to me that I might even be remotely interested in becoming a minister. That was something just *not* on my radar. But the gnostic beliefs and principles were a balm and a bright light, all at the same time. They soothed places in me I didn't even know needed healing. I wanted to be able to help other people who had also suffered with the fire-and-brimstone philosophy of the church. I wanted them to know there was another belief system, one that was more open and compassionate. There was an alternative to mainstream religion.

During the training program we were also exposed to the idea of past lives and the ability we all have to learn more about them. This wasn't something I had ever given much thought, and if I had I would likely have been skeptical. Who knew that training to be a minister would involve a past-life regression while under hypnosis? But it did, and it's an experience that changed the course of my life.

One of the Novus Spiritus hypnotists, Ian Winston, came to Calgary to give our community more information about the concept of past lives. About 35 of us had gathered, and Ian presented his talk before offering to do a group regression for audience members. I was open to the idea but had no idea if anything would happen. I was hopeful and nervous at the same time.

Using techniques to relax us, Ian asked us to let our logical minds rest and just trust whatever it was we saw or heard or experienced, with no judgment. I remember him saying, "Just pay attention and observe and be aware." As soon as I did this, I could see myself standing in a farmer's field. I looked at my feet and could see I was wearing boots with brown pants, and a white, puffy shirt with the sleeves rolled up. I had white skin and dirty-blond hair that hung past my shoulders, tied in a ponytail. I also saw that I had a tool in my hand, and I knew I was using it for my work in the field. I had a feeling it was the 1200s, and that I was in southern France. I also knew I was a Christian, but I wasn't Catholic. I didn't know how I knew any of these things.

I looked behind me and saw a castle upon a hill. To my right was a little, elongated building, and in the middle was a blacksmith's work area. A man was hammering on a piece of metal, and sparks were flying off. He had a dark mustache and curly salt-and-pepper hair. His large belly was covered by a leather apron, and there was a fire blazing behind him. As I watched he looked up at me and smiled. I didn't expect to recognize him, but I did! At that moment, which felt very surreal, I knew this blacksmith was my father. Not only my father in that life, but in this one as well. It was the same person, even though they looked completely different.

Suddenly, something else happened that caught my attention. On another hill, about half a kilometer away, a switchback road zigzagged down from the top. Something white caught my eye. It looked as though a white horse was running down the hill, and as it got closer, I could see there was a woman astride the horse. She was dressed completely in white, and had long, flowing blond hair down to her hips. There was no saddle on her horse, and as she rode to a stop in front of me the very first thing I noticed was how clean she looked. It made me realize that I was quite dirty. I felt attracted to her, but at the same time afraid. I knew I mustn't look her in the eyes, as she seemed like somebody very important—like a princess. Even so, I didn't know who she was so I kept my eyes down and tried to busy myself with the tool in my hands, scraping at the ground. She began to laugh and galloped around me in a circle. I didn't know what to do and felt very awkward. Was I allowed to interact with her? What did she want? And then she was gone, and I was suddenly aware of Ian Winston's voice saying it was time to come back to the room, and to the present time, and to feel ourselves in our bodies again.

I was amazed by what had happened, but also confused. My mind was full of questions, but the biggest was whether I had really just remembered a past life or whether

I had just made the whole thing up. I remember chuckling to myself and thinking I had a pretty vivid imagination. Marissa and I went home that night, and although I knew we were both thinking about what had happened, neither of us talked about it right away. We didn't mention it until the next morning, when she shook me from sleep to say she couldn't stop thinking about her experience and to ask me about mine.

"Mine was odd," she said. "I think it was southern France, around the 1200s, and I was a princess or something. I was riding a horse and there was a castle, and I rode up to this farmer boy in a field. I thought he was really cute, and I started laughing and teasing him. He had dirty-blond hair and was wearing a puffy, pirate-type shirt. When I looked at him I knew it was you! I recognized you even though you looked totally different."

I sat bolt upright in bed. I couldn't believe it! And neither could she, once I explained I had experienced the same in reverse. My logical mind went right to being skeptical, and I felt certain Ian must have made some specific hypnotic suggestions that would explain why we had the same experience. So, I called Ian up to ask if he had instructed us to imagine a life in France in the 1200s— and if he had suggested farmers or castles or horses! Ian assured me none of his suggestions were specific at all. He simply had us relax and instructed us to feel comfortable and open to whatever surfaced.

When I told him about what had happened he was reassuring, and said sometimes couples who had shared past lives would have a similar experience in a past-life regression. I still wasn't convinced. I told him I needed all the phone numbers of the people in class because I intended to call everyone.

I did just that, and not one person's experience was even close to the same as ours. I found this incredibly profound, which was not to say that my logical mind didn't continue to interfere. It did, and I still wasn't completely convinced, but I definitely knew I wanted to find out more and wanted to continue to explore the notion of having lived more than once. At that time I had no idea where this interest in past lives would take me.

CHAPTER 8

Apija'si Kis tliaq~p

TRAVELING BACK IN TIME

Time passed, but I found I couldn't shake the past-life experience. I returned to it over and over in my mind and found myself increasingly curious. I needed to know whether what we had experienced was real or a figment of our imaginations. The fact Marissa had experienced the same life in the regression gave the event further validity, and she, too, was interested in finding out more.

We did research on life in southern France during the 1200s and discovered there was a group of non-Catholic Christians who lived in that region. To my delight and amazement, they were gnostics! The faith was called Catharism. If I truly had lived the life of that farmer boy, this may explain the deep resonance I felt with the gnostic-based teachings of the Novus Spiritus Church.

I also learned, in the early 1200s the Cathars mostly resided in and around Languedoc in southern France, and many of their castles were still standing. My wife and I started to talk about the prospect of actually going to France, as we felt the need to experience the region first-hand and see what we felt when we actually stepped foot on the land. When we learned the literal meaning of Languedoc is "language of yes," it pushed us over the edge and we began to make this dream of ours a reality.

After four days in Paris, we made our way to Espéraza, the heart of Cathar country. Many of the famous Cathar sites, including the castles, were only a short drive away. With only nine days in the area, the question was which ones we should visit. The task ahead seemed overwhelming, but I had an inner certainty we would find what we were looking for—and when we did, we'd know it.

We checked in to our quaint bed-and-breakfast overlooking the Aude River and were delighted to find our hosts, a French couple, spoke excellent English. We told them the story of our shared past life, discovered through hypnotic regression, and asked if they had ever heard legends about a "lady in white," or a princess, who rode horseback. They hadn't, but the man was quite knowledgable about the Cathars and was able to recommend some castles he thought we should visit.

On our large map of the area, he circled five castles, all of which had been around in the early 1200s. He recommended Château de Quéribus, Peyrepertuse, Puivert, Montségur, and the large Cathar castle in Carcassonne, the city where we'd picked up the car. We made an itinerary for our remaining days in France, planning to visit at least one castle per day.

Two days and two castles later, we went back to Carcassonne. The massive, double-walled castle actually housed an entire town—called La Cité—inside of it. There is quite a history to this enormous Cathar relic: it's the place where the crusading army surrounded the castle and forced a surrender. Initiated by the Catholic Church to eliminate Catharism, the castle was ruled by Raymond Roger Trencavel, a lord in the region. He was not a Cathar but was of the belief that Cathars and Catholics could live harmoniously together. There was even a Catholic Church in La Cité.

When I heard Trencavel's name it instantly felt familiar, like I'd known him before, but I wasn't connecting to anything in the castle itself. I felt very sorrowful about what happened in that place, but it didn't feel like where I had lived as the farmer boy. When we left Carcassonne that day I was starting to wonder if we were ever going to find our past home. With all the Cathar Castles in the region the quest began to feel a little bit like searching for a needle in a haystack. I remember driving back to our bed-and-breakfast that evening and wondering as we passed other Cathar Castles if any of them contained the answer.

The next day dawned clear and hot. There were only two castles left on our list: Puivert and Montségur. We decided to travel to Montségur first because of its pivotal place in the history of the Cathars, and then on our way back would take in Puivert.

The Château de Montségur is probably the best known of all the Cathar Castles. Its name literally means "safe hill," and for a time the 1,200-meter-high castle, poised atop a rocky mountain, was just that for the scores of dispossessed Cathar families seeking shelter from the Catholic Crusaders.

In 1243, a siege began at Montségur and 10,000 Royal Catholic troops surrounded the castle. The Pope had ordered the Cathars to convert to Catholicism or be killed. A pyre was erected at the bottom of the mountain. Inside, however, the Cathars had immense stores of food and water, and were able to hold out for 10 months. When their resources became depleted, in March of 1244, the Cathars announced they would surrender, but wanted a 15-day truce. This gave them time to celebrate the spring equinox one last time.

On March 16, 1244, the last Cathars exited Montségur. It is said the just over 200 residents linked hands, sang, and marched down the mountain. Of the 200,000 Cathars of France, they were all that was left after the Crusades. When they reached the bottom of the mountain, every single one walked straight into the burning fire.

I thought of this incredibly moving story as Montségur came into view, of the Cathars who had held out to the end and who would rather die than renounce what they believed. These amazing people would rather have been burned alive than live a lie. I found their story so inspiring and, more than that, I felt an intense connection to this land and to these people. We stopped at the bottom of the mountain, where the pyre would have been, and found a tombstone with an inscription that read: *The Cathars, martyrs of pure Christian love. 16 March 1244.* I picked some wildflowers and laid them on the grave before beginning our ascent up the mountain. It was incredibly steep, but when we reached the top we were rewarded with an unbelievable view that stretched almost to the sea, hundreds of kilometers away. There was a French tour going on inside and because we couldn't understand, Marissa and I wandered around on our own. We walked slowly, exploring both the inside and the outside, getting a real feel for the place. There was a sense of deep familiarity, and I was moved to tears numerous times that day.

Leaving Montségur, we headed back toward our inn, stopping at the last Cathar castle on our list. Puivert looked nothing like the others. First of all, it was built at the top of a small hill, not a mountaintop. Second, it had the same turrets and towers, but its shape was more a square than a rectangle. As we drove up to the parking area Puivert seemed the most familiar to me, yet something was still a little off.

At the front gate, where there was a drawbridge entrance to the castle, a dark-haired young man sat at a kiosk, selling books and postcards and giving out pamphlets. Something nudged me to talk to him, and we discovered he spoke very good English. I told him how we'd been searching everywhere for stories about a woman in white, possibly a princess, who lived during the time of the Cathars. As I began to list off the places we'd been, he interrupted.

"I know exactly who you're talking about," he said.

"You do?" I exclaimed. Marissa and I exchanged looks of excitement.

"Yeah, I work here in the summer, but I'm a student majoring in history. I love the history of the Cathars." My heart was pounding as he continued. "There is a legend about the Lady in White here at Puivert, from the 13th century. It is said she was a princess in Aragon, Spain, and she was known for riding bareback on a white horse. She is said to have had long blond hair."

Breathless, we urged him on.

"The castle was best known for the traveling troubadours who would visit once a year and play music and recite poetry. The legend goes that one year all the farmers' fields flooded, and the troubadours could not come. The Lady in White loved the troubadours and was very distressed. She had a special rock where she prayed and went there to ask that the waters recede so the musicians and poets could return. On the day the water disappeared, the Lady in White did as well, and was never seen or heard from again. The legend goes on to say she had given her life, or thrown herself into the water, to save the land and ensure the troubadours could return."

I had gone from being discouraged, imagining we would have to return home without any answers, to absolute elation. This was feeling very right, but something still didn't make sense. "If this was the right place, why did the castle look unfamiliar?" I asked our young guide.

"Probably because it's been rebuilt many times!" he responded. "Come, I'll show you. The original castle is back here." He led us around the backside of the castle, which was mostly in ruins. As I walked around, I saw the original imprints of pictures carved into the stone walls. They depicted musicians and large gatherings of people, and looked familiar to me. We walked through all the old rooms and then up the spiral stone staircase, which led to the tower at the back of the castle, and into a turret.

I looked out onto the land below and across to the hill. The same zigzagging road cut through it, and I knew we had found the right place. As if to underscore the point, as I looked down into the fields, the young man said, "Puivert was a farming community that helped supply food for Carcassonne and the lands of Raymond Roger Trencavel. He was the lord of this land."

Goose bumps broke out all over my body. That's why Trencavel's name had felt so familiar. I practically flew down the narrow spiral staircase in my haste to get out to the fields below. I needed to stand in the exact spot I had as a farmer boy. As if being pulled by a magnet, I walked quickly until stopping at what felt like the right place. From there I could see the castle on the hill, and to my right were the ruins of the blacksmith shop. Just as it had been in my regression.

I knew at that moment, with absolute certainty, the past life Marissa and I had experienced together had been very real. There was no doubt in my mind that I had lived here and that I had once stood in this very spot.

Eight hundred years later, I had returned home.

CHAPTER 9

Wikatikene'l Kinu'a'taqnn Na'kwek, Jijaqmije'l Kisi Piskiaq

PAPER MESSAGES BY DAY, SPIRIT BY NIGHT

Sometime after Marissa and I had returned from France, we began to notice the fabric of our Calgary neighborhood shifting and changing, and not for the better. There was a real rise in crime and gang activity, which began to be felt in the area where we lived and made me feel less and less comfortable in this ever-expanding Alberta city. I thought often of how safe Nova Scotia had felt when I was growing up and began to wonder if it might be possible for me to move my family back.

There were no transfer opportunities within the company where I worked, and although I was making money from my readings it certainly wasn't enough to support a family. I realized that in order to return to the Maritimes I would need a new career. One day, while I was heading home from work and feeling the weight of responsibility, I decided I needed help. I decided to call on the universe. *Please help me figure out a way to get home to Nova Scotia*, I implored. At that exact moment a Canada Post truck drove by, and a light bulb went on.

Working for Canada Post would be perfect. Plus, the fact my great-great-grandfather had been one of the first postmasters in Canada felt like a great sign. I applied for a temporary position with Canada Post and immediately got three days of work. Soon after—due to a series of events involving me going to the head of HR without an interview—I got a permanent position.

On the day I was notified of my full-time, permanent status, I applied for a transfer. It took 18 months, but the day finally came; I got the phone call I'd been waiting for. My transfer had been granted, and I would be delivering mail in Halifax. I had two weeks to get there and claim my spot, so I packed our PT Cruiser with some personal items and set off across the country. I was determined to find a home for my family and make a new start in the place I had first called home.

Finally in Nova Scotia, we set about building our lives. I found a place in Hammonds Plains, a small community within easy commuting distance to Halifax that had lots of space for our kids to play outside. After living in a huge city, a place where I had come to fear for my children's safety, being back home felt comforting and secure. Marissa and the kids soon joined me, and we all settled in.

Word of mouth followed me back to Nova Scotia, and I began to again book evening readings. Although we were in a new place, my life as I knew it resumed: I delivered paper messages by day, and spirit messages by night. I'd even built a little office beside the house to keep the business separate from home. I thought it would help my wife with some of her increasing worries about my work as a medium. Before we left Calgary I'd done some work for the police, and it had become public. Marissa was very uncomfortable with the possibility that one of the criminals I'd given information on knew my name, and would be able to find our family.

In order to build up the same solid client base I'd had in Calgary, I knew I would need to get out and start meeting people. My ultimate goal was to one day be able to leave Canada Post and work solely as a medium. To do that I needed to become known for my abilities in Nova Scotia. After all, although I'd grown up in the province, I'd never worked here as a medium.

I discovered a local spiritualist church where people were conducting readings. I went to check them out and quickly knew this was the next step for my career. I'd been doing individual readings for many years, and through my minister training I'd gained some valuable experience talking to groups. I offered the group my services as a medium and told them about my background in the Novus Spiritus tradition. I needed to see if the work of connecting with Spirit and allowing their messages to come through could be done while standing in front of a group.

My first experience was with a small group of around 30 people, and as I had already gotten to know a few of them it didn't feel as though I were facing a room full of strangers. I first gave a talk about my experiences connecting with Spirit, and then it was time to see who came through. This involves flipping a switch in my mind, where I go from speaking to a form of deep listening. It's necessary for my awareness to shift from the external world to my own internal world, where I can see, feel, hear, and allow those internal senses to guide. Only then can I give the messages to those waiting. Up until that moment I didn't have any experience doing this in front of a group, but I found that the process was the same.

I tuned in and immediately began to see drumsticks. I felt this message was coming from a father who had passed and was meant for his son, who was in the room. I voiced this and a young man spoke up.

"I'm a drummer, and I design mallets for drums."

Bingo. "Okay, this is for you then. Your father is coming through. I feel like he hasn't passed all that long ago. He's showing me a place where you used to walk together. It looks like Point Pleasant Park."

The man nodded slowly, tears in his eyes.

"He wants you to know he still walks there with you."

The young man went on to explain that he and his father would take walks at the park during the last year of his life. The son still walked there, and often thought of his dad.

"When you're thinking of him like that, he's right there with you. You're not just remembering. He's there and he wants you to know that."

The spiritualist church asked me to come back again and I did, to increasing numbers of people each week.

Doing these small readings was a great way to build my confidence, but something was going on behind the scenes of which I wasn't aware. Apparently, a few of the other mediums in the church had begun to spread rumors about me that weren't true, but they elicited the attention of the head minister, a woman from Montreal. She came to investigate and ended up firing the other mediums for spreading lies.

The experience helped me learn a valuable lesson, similar to the one I'd learned through Novus Spiritus. Simply put, being involved in any organization where ego and competition are in play just isn't a place for me. I realized with crystal-like clarity that I didn't need to be part of a group or a team or a religion. I just had to be me—my own person—and focus on the work I felt a deep call to do. This work was about helping people heal their lives and move beyond grief; helping them to see their loved ones are still with them, just in a different form, and are fully able to communicate.

That was the end of my membership in organizations, although my involvement in both Novus Spiritus and the spiritualist church helped me grow as both a medium and a person.

CHAPTER 10

Nato'q Tla'sitew
THY WILL BE DONE

I often sense information on a psychic level that isn't always easy to process. I've had to learn to create boundaries with the spirit world so that I receive only messages that would allow me to prevent moments of catastrophe, otherwise I can be left feeling helpless if I am unable to prevent tragic events from taking place. Over the years I've learned a lot and come to realize that some of the messages I receive are great teaching tools—not only for others but also for myself, and one such event took place shortly after I returned to Nova Scotia.

After we relocated to Hammonds Plains after many years in Calgary, I was able to reconnect with my mother. She had missed all of us, especially her grandkids, and we made a point to spend more time together. My mom had remarried the year I moved to Calgary, and her new husband, Larry, was a great guy. Like my dad, Larry had also worked for the military and was a former air force captain.

He was hardworking, loyal, kind, and helpful. He was also analytical and methodical—a "measure twice, cut once" kind of guy—and had doubts about my work as a spirit talker. I surprised him one day when his mom came through to me loud and clear. I said her name, which I hadn't known, and he asked, "How would you know that?" I laughed and said, "This is what I do."

Every so often I would surprise him with a little piece of information that there was no way I would have known. His mom told me how she used to make his favorite pudding. So, I made him some sticky toffee pudding—in the same way his mother used to make it—the next time he was over. He gave me a confused look, and I responded simply with, "I just know, Larry."

One day, he came over to help hang my clothesline. While he was there, he complained about a headache. I gave him some Tylenol and didn't think twice about it, but later in the day a strange thing happened. As he left the garage to go back inside the house, I noticed a dark mass at the base of his skull. It was there for only a moment and then gone again, yet the image stayed with me the rest of the day. I couldn't shake what I saw, and I didn't want to believe what I had seen.

The following weekend my daughter had a highland dance recital, and I expected to see Larry there. My mom said that he couldn't make it because he still had that "damn headache" and expressed that she was worried about him because he had been struggling with it for more than a week, and no matter how much medication he seemed to take the pain wouldn't go away.

She seemed concerned, and I decided to tell her everything that I had seen. I said, "I don't want to scare you but last week I saw something on the back of Larry's head. I wanted it to be nothing, so I didn't tell anyone, and I still hope that I'm wrong, but I think you should get him checked out right away."

My mom left immediately and took Larry to the hospital. The doctors did a scan and found a mass in the back of Larry's brain stem, and he was scheduled for surgery two days later when it was revealed that the tumors were cancerous. The tests also indicated that the cancer hadn't originated in the brain, and after the full-body scan was performed, we were informed that the cancer was in most of Larry's organs and had traveled all the way up his spine. The brain was the last place the cancer took hold, and he was long past the point of recovery.

I was angry when I heard the news. I was angry with myself because I'm supposed to see those kinds of things; I should be able to help the people I love. I was angry with the spirit world. I was so disappointed that by the time I was shown that there was cancer, it was too late. I struggled with why Spirit would show me now, and not sooner, when something could have been done to save him.

After we were given the devastating news Larry went downhill quickly, and I spent a lot of time at their house trying to make up for lost time. I wanted to connect with the man to better understand his journey, and perhaps help him in some way. In those last couple of months Larry was open and curious, and I was more than happy to reveal what I knew to be true about what it's like to make our journeys home.

I told him that "When it's your time, when you're passing over, you're going to see a beautiful white light." He laughed it off and responded with, "That's just an old wives' tale. When it's over, its lights out!" I softly told him, "I've seen it myself, and I can guarantee it will be the most incredible thing you have ever seen."

At this point in time he became very quiet but didn't take his eyes off me. I continued, "When you see it, I want you to go toward the light. That is our true home, and where we all come from." I paused and could see tears in his eyes. "Do you really think I'll see the light, Shawn?" I explained, "I don't just think it; I *know* it."

The certainty of my words and how I expressed them to Larry gave him comfort, and I felt happy that I could play a role in the final days of this good man's life. What I wanted most was to facilitate healing so that Larry and my mom could have a few more years together, a few more trips to their cabin in Newfoundland, and a few more fishing expeditions. Although his diagnosis was grim, we tried praying with good intentions, positive thinking, and hands-on healing, but despite it all and within only two months of the surgery, Larry passed away. At the time the only consolation was that he appeared not to have suffered too much.

He had decided that he didn't want to die at home, and I had visited with them on the evening before he passed away. In the middle of the night Larry suddenly awoke and yelled out, "Truro," which is the name of the town where the hospital is located, and he collapsed immediately after he spoke out his request. He knew the time had come, and thankfully the ambulance arrived quickly. Unfortunately, the door frames were too narrow for the stretcher, and I had to carry him into the ambulance. When I picked Larry up, he weighed only about 75 pounds, and as I laid him onto the stretcher I reminded him of the light, and I also made a special request.

"Larry, I know that you can hear me, and I want you to do something for me. I want you to send me a sign, so that I know you found the light and you made it home, okay?" The next morning my mom called from the hospital to say that he had passed away on September 11, 2011.

I know he heard my request, and he didn't wait long to answer me.

My wife, my aunt Patsy, my children, and I all got into my car and headed to the hospital. I told Patsy, who was staying with us at the time, what I asked Larry to do, and I said that I knew we were going to get a sign from him shortly. A few minutes later I spotted an eagle and I said, "Do you see that, Patsy?" She responded with, "Yeah, I see that, but it's just an eagle." Even though the eagle was high above us I was certain it was a sign from Larry, which is why I was the only one who was not completely surprised when the eagle suddenly dropped from the sky and dive-bombed our car.

I was driving 100 kilometers per hour, and this eagle not only aimed itself toward our vehicle, but as it came closer it turned sideways and swept across the whole front of the windshield. Its wings were fully spread, and the tip of one lightly touched the pavement. I had to press hard on the brakes, or I would have hit and killed this magnificent creature.

I watched as the eagle soared back into the sky as my heart thumped in my chest. I asked, "Do you think it's just an eagle now?" And my aunt Patsy burst into tears and cried out, "Oh my God. That was the most spiritual experience I have ever had in my whole life." I immediately thanked Larry and couldn't help but chuckle to myself over the intensity of his message.

A few days later I spoke at his funeral and read the Lord's Prayer, and it wasn't until I returned home that I understood why things had unfolded the way they did for Larry, and why I was unable to save him. My mom had asked me to say this prayer and these words, which I had done out of respect for both Larry and her. I spoke the words she requested me to speak even though I have a different take on the interpretation of the text, since they had been translated several times before the English translation ever hit the printing press.

I had never felt a resonance to the Lord's Prayer and felt that it never really spoke to me, but on the day of his funeral, as I read the words, I was struck by a certain line in the text. The words "thy will be done" resonated differently for me that day, and have every day since. It was in that moment I realized no matter how much we prayed or did healing work on Larry's body, the cancer was not meant to be healed.

It reconfirmed to me that no matter how much we may pray, or what words we speak, or how badly we want something—some aspects of our lives are charted and cannot be changed. Our prayers are always heard by those who love and guide us from the spirit world. I learned that no matter how we think life should unfold, everyone has their time here, but when it's your time to return home, there's no way to change that. When we pray to the Creator, or whatever you choose to call God, Jesus, a higher power, etc., the greater good is always taken into consideration when divine intervention comes into play, and how those prayers are answered.

Some events in the physical world cannot be changed. Long before we ever incarnated here in this life, they were charted, part of a grand, planned design. There is no way to change what is meant to happen. I learned this lesson with my father, James, and that there was a reason for his untimely passing, and that his death couldn't have been avoided. There are greater intended purposes behind the will of the Creator, and changes can occur only when that alteration is in alignment with the greater good of everyone involved.

CHAPTER 11

APOQNMASUTI WEJIAQ A'SE'K

SUPPORT FROM THE OTHER SIDE

After Larry's funeral, the dust settled somewhat. Our family continued to adjust to life in a new province, but it was becoming more and more obvious my wife and I weren't happy in our relationship. While I spent an increasing amount of time thinking about how I could quit my job and transition to doing the work I loved full time, she wanted me to put less focus on mediumship. I truly believed I was helping to heal hearts, and the idea of spending whole days doing this beautiful and meaningful work felt as though I was fulfilling my soul's true purpose.

Unfortunately, fear got in the way. Fear told me I should stay in my relationship and stay with my work as a mail carrier. I was afraid of what divorce would mean for our kids, and I was afraid of not having enough money. In those days, fear was keeping me small and not allowing me to become who I was meant to be.

It was during this time I had a few physical encounters with the spirit world that solidified the notion that working with Spirit really was my life's calling. These experiences also changed what I had known, up to that point, about how Spirit can appear and connect.

I was delivering mail in the Hydrostone area of Halifax and walked up the steps of an office building. I hadn't seen anyone at the top, but when I got there a man was holding the door open. He looked just like my great-uncle Rob, but maybe 40 years younger. A good-looking, vibrant, healthy, and happy man—smiling at me from ear to ear. I was quite struck by the resemblance to my great-uncle, and also by the presence of this man. He seemed to be standing there just for me, smiling and attentive. I thanked him and walked through the door, and as I did my phone rang.

"Did you hear the news?" It was my mother. "Your great-uncle Rob passed."

Oh my God. It *was* him. I ran to the door and flew back down the stairs, scanning up and down the street. He was gone. Completely vanished.

"Shawn? Are you there?"

"Yeah, yeah. I'm here." I stood on the street, shaking my head and marveling at it all.

"Mom, you're not going to believe this, but I'm pretty sure I just saw Uncle Rob. He just held the door open for me at a building on Kaye Street. It was him, letting me know he's okay; that he's better than okay, actually."

It wasn't until I hung up that I remembered the last time I saw my great-uncle Rob had been at Larry's funeral. He was in a wheelchair, hooked up to an oxygen machine. Rob was my mom's uncle and had been a heavy smoker his whole life. He'd been diagnosed with lung cancer and the prognosis wasn't good. Although he was in his late 70s he looked older when I saw him, a small and shriveled version of who he had been.

"Rob, you shouldn't be here," I had said, bending low over the wheelchair and taking his hand.

"I couldn't miss saying good-bye to Larry," he whispered hoarsely. "My time's coming soon, Shawn. I have to be okay with this."

I squeezed his hand. "I probably won't get to see you again, but I want to ask you something. When you go, can you please visit me?"

"I will." His eyes glistened with tears.

It was my turn to choke back my emotions. "And when you get there, please tell Larry I said hi and I love him."

We parted ways after one last hug, and one last look into each other's eyes. Now here I was, standing on the street on a sunny day in Halifax, phone in hand, in awe at what had happened. He'd done it; my Uncle Rob was good to his word. And he hadn't found just any old way to communicate with me—he hadn't sent a feather or an eagle or a song on the radio—he'd sent himself! A version many decades younger, looking strong and cheerful and happy. He had paid me a most extraordinary visit, on the very day he passed from this earth, clearly showing me how well he now was.

This experience left me reeling, and also fascinated and newly curious about all the ways Spirit can communicate with us. It occurred to me, in those days after seeing the flesh and blood version of Uncle Rob, that there is really no limit to how Spirit communicates and shows up for us. It's only our own beliefs about what is possible and not possible that stop them sometimes from appearing.

Seeing Uncle Rob was the first time since becoming a medium that a spirit had visited in the human form. It got me thinking about my early childhood and my spirit guide Sam, and about how real he had been despite the fact no one else could see him. I also recalled how my great-grandparents were once present in physical form in my childhood bed during the night, how their "realness" had scared me.

I then started thinking about how nice it would be to see my great-grandparents again, and the experience with Rob made me realize this was possible. A few weeks later, walking down another street in Halifax delivering mail, an older gentleman appeared in front of me from out of nowhere. I had been starting up a walkway when suddenly, on this quiet street, there was a man who looked an awful lot like my great-grandfather.

"I'll take that for you," he said.

I must have looked at him curiously because he repeated himself. "I'll put that in the mailbox for you."

My gut was telling me I was having another "Uncle Rob" moment; there was something quite surreal about this encounter. Still, my logical brain questioned it. *This guy must just live here,* I thought, giving my head a shake. I handed him the mail and turned to leave. The only thing was, as I walked away, I didn't hear the door and I didn't hear the mail slot. I turned around. He was gone. It was exactly the same thing that happened with Uncle Rob. This older man had completely disappeared, in the space of about three seconds.

If you take anything from this chapter, I would like it to be this: trust yourself. We all have ideas of what spirit connection and communication looks like, sometimes largely based on books or movies concerning ghosts, but they're not all wispy beings who walk through walls. I can tell you with certainty that some are as physical as you and me. There's a Bible verse from the Old Testament that is especially apt here: "Be not forgetful to entertain strangers: for thereby some have entertained angels unawares." (King James Version, Hebrews 13:2.)

If you think back over your life, you'll probably remember certain encounters with strangers that have been meaningful in some way. Perhaps someone said something that altered a course of thinking for the better. Maybe you were delayed while in a hurry, only to realize the delay saved you from a car accident. We simply cannot know how often Spirit is communing with us, or in what ways, but I'd like to encourage you to be open to how you are being guided and supported.

I know, without a doubt, we all have people watching over us, so the next time you have an odd encounter on the street or in the grocery store—something that feels a little bit surreal or supernatural—do yourself a favor and turn around when the other person walks away. They may have just vanished into the light! And then you'll know.

MEDITATION ON OPENING UP AND BEING GUIDED AND SUPPORTED

Please sit or lie in a comfortable space and location, where you will not be disturbed.

Ask the Creator and Ancestors to surround you with an unconditional loving light of divine guidance and protection.

Close your eyes and take three, slow deep breaths.

Now envision yourself with your psychic inner eyes, walking down a beautiful well-lit pathway through the forest.

Smell the air and freshness of the grass and trees that surround you.

Feel the warm gentle breeze that touches your skin.

In the distance you will now see a figure that may be hard to make out at first, although as this person gets closer you can see it is a specific family member in the spirit world or maybe a spiritual guide.

Whoever it is, trust your first impression.

Embrace this person with an open heart and spirit.

Give them a hug and stand back, and ask them to help you be more in alignment with your highest spiritual purpose in this lifetime.

Give them permission to appear within your physical life and guide you in such a way that all will be obvious and clear.

Ask them for their unique sign for you.

Hug them and thank them heart to heart.

Step back, close your psychic eyes, and count yourself up—one, two, three.

Take a deep breath and come fully back and fully conscious.

Open your physical eyes, feeling better than you have in a long, long time.

CHAPTER 12

WELTESKUJ JIJAQMIJEY ILA'KWENAWETE'W

MEETING YOUR SPIRIT GUIDE

While my wife and I definitely had a strong past-life connection, it became clear to both of us we weren't meant to be married to each other for our whole lives. We decided to separate and, soon after, divorced. I truly believe Marissa and I were meant to learn from each other in this life, and I'm grateful for all the experiences and all the love we shared—even the hard times.

After our separation there were, of course, many logistics to work out. I needed to find another place to live, and we needed to come up with a schedule that worked for the kids. Once everything was finally in place I began to feel a renewed sense of movement and possibility in my life. I felt free to make decisions I felt were good for me. The biggest way this manifested was being able to start putting more energy into the work I really loved. This meant I began to follow both my heart and my intuition when it came to my work as a psychic medium.

I strongly felt the urge to start doing live shows, even though I had a good amount of fear at the thought. What if I couldn't read people in a large group? What if I got up there and nothing happened? I had already proven to myself I could do readings in small group gatherings, like the ones at the local spiritualist church. There I had received valuable, clear information and validation that Spirit was ready to communicate, even in a group setting. I had long been drawn to trying this out with a much larger group, and in the wake of suddenly being on my own I saw no reason not to try.

I brought in a guy I'd grown up with, Darrell, to help with the organization. Word of mouth was spreading about who I was and what I did, and we ended up selling 85 tickets. I was happy about the amount of people, and although I was nervous, the event went really well. The connections with Spirit were solid, and afterward I received inspiring messages from a number of people. I even got some good press and social media exposure.

The success of this first show seemed like a sign from the Great Spirit that I didn't need to worry about clinging to the security of my Canada Post job. Freed from some of the fears, which had been my constant over the last few years, I began to trust in my abilities more and believe in the guidance I received. In fact, it was during this time I became acquainted with a guide I didn't know I had—one who would help me face more of my fears and begin to walk more fully into my destiny.

She came to me in a dream. I appeared to be in Scotland, and in the dream a beautiful barefoot woman, wearing an intricately designed white gown, descended a hill by a river and came toward me.

She wasn't very tall, probably about five foot two or three, and had dark hair and stunningly beautiful, light-filled eyes. I felt a loving, confident, strong, and determined energy emitting from her. Her presence instantly made me feel safe. "Shawn, I am Victoria," she said, a Gaelic lilt to her voice.

"I want you to know I'm going to be helping you from now on with the work you're doing." I knew she wasn't talking about my job as a letter carrier!

"Are you a new guide?" I asked her.

"I've always been here, but I've not been working much with you. You need me now more than ever, so I will become more present." She went on to explain she would be my guide for all the work I was doing, connecting to spirits and different levels of energy. Victoria promised to protect me during this journey, and when she said that I felt very, very safe.

"Well, thank you. It's nice to meet you," I said. I then promptly woke up, the Scotland scene vanishing from sight, but I was left with a feeling of excitement at this new connection.

This amazing encounter felt so very real, and I didn't doubt for a second Victoria was at my side. I began to have an inner dialogue with her, and strongly felt her directing me to seek out spiritual wisdom via books and spiritual writers. I believe Victoria led me to authors like Wayne Dyer, Anita Moorjani, and Eckhart Tolle. Expanding my wisdom base gave me a new vocabulary that enabled me to help people in deeper ways, giving them a kind of tangible and practical guidance. Finding out about a new guide also made me more eager than ever to bring my childhood friend Sam back into my conscious awareness. It didn't take much for him to make his presence known.

I began doing daily spirit guide meditation with the intent and purpose to connect with Sam. These guided meditations were relaxing, so I sometimes fell asleep. I remember telling Sam that if I fell asleep, I wanted him to wake me up, but I was still not expecting for someone, just as I was drifting off, to grab my arm, pick it up, and drop it on the bed. That was amazing enough, but what came next really blew me away. It was as though I were watching a stone being dropped into a pond and witnessing the subsequent ripples fanning out. Intense, tingling energy spread from my arm and all the way through my body. I had never felt anything like it. It was like light poured through me, touching every cell and every fiber of my being. In that moment I saw Sam's face and he smiled at me, light sparkling through both of us. I knew he had been there all along, and whenever I needed him in the future, I knew he would still be right there.

All of us have guides, and all of us have the ability to connect with them. If you're interested in finding out more about your guides—including their names—talk to them and ask them to communicate with you. Practice meditation with the intention of connecting to your guides. Tell them you'd like the chance to hear them, see them, and experience them. Tell them you are open and receptive to any form of communication, including dreams, thoughts, or messages you hear out in the world. For example, you may begin noticing the same name repeated over and over in different circles. This may be your guide's way of saying, "Hey, that's me!" Sam and Victoria are very special, and hugely important in my life. I feel their support and guidance every day. I know with absolute certainty none of us are ever alone, and it's a great gift when we all realize this. Once you experience the kind of love our spirit guides have for us, you'll never feel alone again.

MEETING YOUR SPIRIT GUIDE

When you're ready to connect to a spiritual guide, talk to them out loud and tell them you are ready to reconnect in such a way that you will know who they are.

Knowing who they are is nice, but it is not needed to speak to your guides. Just speaking out loud to your guides is all that is needed for them to hear you and respond to helping you in profound ways. You can also meditate with the sincere intention of meeting your guide.

If you would like to meet one or more of your guides in a dream, tell them that you wish to reconnect in this way. Invite them into your dreams!

Eventually, they will find an opening in your dreams to connect. I am sure they have always been there, as they are typically the friend that is with you in your dreams that you can't quite make out.

No matter what, talk to your guides; they will hear you and have always been there waiting for you to remember that they are there.

CHAPTER 13

KIWALSIAQEWE'L TELITPIEMK~L PARANORMAL EXPERIENCES

I was having more and more experiences that served to expand my understanding of what form Spirit can take, and how Spirit communicates. I felt hungry to explore this area further, so when I was invited to join a paranormal group in Halifax I leapt at the chance.

I had my own ideas about what was happening with the spirits I could connect to—namely, that they were choosing not to move into the light of the higher level of the spirit world. This, I believe, is the one place we are all meant to ascend to after we vacate our human physical body. For whatever reason, however, some spirits do not choose to transition. I call this in-between place they inhabit the astral world. This is where I believe some people get lost or stuck, perhaps due to fear or self-judgment.

From what I've witnessed, those who get stuck on the earth plane are very much still entrenched within their egotistical self, and usually inhabit the same place they lived—or died.

Such was the case with the spirit of the pirate we encountered during one of my very first outings with the paranormal group. We went to Point Pleasant Park at nighttime with a film crew and sat at a picnic table near the Prince of Wales Tower. As I was about to address the group, I heard my spirit guide Victoria clearly say, "They will be no good." I knew she was warning me the spirits we would connect to at the park were earthbound spirits who have chosen not to move into the light. I heard her warning and felt thankful for her presence, but I was still intrigued to find out more about who was there. As the leader of the group, I led us in a spirit circle, where everyone held hands—left hand facing up, right hand facing down. This is a way to intentionally and communally connect our energies and help bridge the gap between this world and the other.

After Victoria sounded her warning, which had come as a mere whisper, she began talking in such a loud voice I initially believed one of the other women at the table was speaking. After a few minutes of confusion, I realized it was Victoria. She was repeating a single word I wasn't familiar with and didn't understand. It sounded like "kidge" or "kedge." Although no one else in the circle could hear her, Victoria's voice was easily recorded on the digital recorders we brought.

It didn't take long to feel someone else around us, and the feeling wasn't very friendly or welcoming. This sense was soon confirmed when I asked aloud if the spirit was connected to this place. I heard the most bloodcurdling growl, as if the spirit had bent low right over my ear. It sounded like the devil himself! I nearly jumped off the picnic table and was surprised to hear the cameraman sitting beside me say, "What the hell was that?"

Later we talked and he admitted to also having heard the growl; he was so terrified he nearly dropped the camera and ran! I, too, was certainly frightened, but with Victoria on my team I knew I was protected—a power she was soon to show firsthand.

"Who are you?" I asked. "Are you connected to this building?"

No further growls met my question, but I could feel the energy of this spirit. I began to have a mental image, and he looked very much like what one may think of as a pirate. The name Edward suddenly came through. At the same moment the woman across from me yelled, "Somebody just grabbed me!"

Over the course of the next 30 minutes nearly everyone at the table felt they were either grabbed or pushed by the spirit, myself included. I could actually feel his fingers gripping my wrist. I knew he was trying to scare us and wanted us to leave.

I repeated myself. "Are you from this place? Are you connected to this building?" Again, I heard my guide say the same words as before: "Go to the kedge."

What happened next was caught on film: the spirit put his hand on my back and pushed. When looking at the footage you can see his handprint on the back of my jacket, and you can see how I am pushed forward by this invisible hand.

Also on the tape is the voice of Victoria, saying sternly, "Get off Shawn." And he did. At that point, and on Victoria's urging, I asked the Creator and the Great Spirit to surround us all with unconditional loving, white light. I instantly felt the energy of the place change, and could feel a collective and relieved sigh around the table. I could no longer feel the energy of the pirate's spirit. Later I wondered if our gathering there, and bringing the light, finally helped him transition and move on.

That night in Point Pleasant Park remains the most vivid paranormal experience I've ever had. And bolstered by what I discovered, I did a little research after the fact. Turns out, there was a man by the name of Edward Jordan who was born in Ireland in 1771 and took part in the Irish rebellions of 1797–98. He was sentenced to death but turned informant and was pardoned. Jordan attempted to start a new life in Nova Scotia as a fisherman, but had mounting debt. The merchants sent Captain John Stairs to seize Jordan's fishing schooner, which was in the Gaspé. Stairs offered Jordan and his wife safe passage back to Halifax, but on the trip back in September of 1809 Jordan tried to take his ship back and slaughtered the crew. Unbeknownst to Jordan, the captain survived and was rescued by a passing fishing schooner. Stairs told the authorities, and Jordan was tried. Found guilty, he was hanged at Black Rock Beach in Point Pleasant Park. His body was tarred, feathered, and hung in a gibbet as a warning to other pirates. His skull still resides at the Maritime Museum of the Atlantic in Halifax.

I discovered the place where people were hanged was where the park's giant iron anchor lay now. Back in Jordan's time, "kedge" was a common word for "anchor."

When she used that word, Victoria was trying to give me a landmark for where the spirit had lost his life.

I do believe our spirits maintain an energetic connection to where we die, so it makes sense this man may still have been haunting this park. I've been back numerous times since that night, but I've never run into him again. I'd like to think we actually did help him move on into the light.

I've had other experiences with spirits who seem to be earthbound and in need of some assistance moving out of their low-level energy place and into the light. Over time, what has become evident is there are also beings—you can call them guides or angels—who are already in the light but are there to help. I encountered one such being soon after my Point Pleasant Park experience.

It was yet another outing with the paranormal group, and we decided to check out McNabs Island, a place in Halifax Harbor with a rich history. The island has numerous forts from various time periods, and so we explored one of the older ruins. We found tunnels leading underground, and as we descended, I became aware of the spirit of a man. He didn't seem frightening in the same way as Edward Jordan. Rather, this spirit seemed more lost and confused. I was attempting to connect with him and encourage him to move toward the light when an amazing thing happened.

A ball of light, also known as an orb, came down through the ceiling. I felt somebody else enter the room. This spirit stood behind me and spoke Mi'kmaq. At one point I actually felt his hand on my back, pushing me hard enough so that I stumbled forward. At the same time, there was a strong and overpowering smell of smoke. I recognized it as burning Sweetgrass and Sage, although there was no visible smoke. It wasn't just me who smelled it! The entire group held our shirts or our hands to our mouths and noses, as the smell was that overpowering. I now know that this new spirit uttered the Mi'kmaq word Msit No'kmaq, which means "all my relations." With that, the spirit who had been trapped disappeared. Just like that.

It was clear to me the spirit who spoke Mi'kmaq, and who put his hand on my back to move me, was an Indigenous Elder from the spirit world. I believe he came to teach me something very important about the power of the light, and about using Indigenous smudging to help earthbound spirits into the light. It was this experience that later led me to seek out a living Indigenous Elder to teach me more about our traditional ways and start to learn more about my own Indigenous Mi'kmaq language. My experiences with the paranormal group taught me a lot about the different realities, or realms, where Spirit can reside. I now understand that humans who die don't always embrace the light and move on. Rather, some remain earthbound due to their fear, in an in-between place, and they have the ability to communicate with us. I also learned there are beings of light helping them to move on, and that we all can play a part in facilitating that movement toward the light.

My thirst for knowledge and deep curiosity about the spirit world, and what I have learned, have made me eager to pass this information on to others. I sincerely hope that any wisdom or knowledge I've gained will help you better understand the spirit world. Because guess what? None of us are getting out of here alive in our physical form, and one day we're all going to end up in the same place: the spirit world.

CHAPTER 14

WELITPA'SIK TEL WULTESKAQ

A CHANCE CONNECTION

When you are in alignment with your life's purpose, situations and circumstances will divinely present themselves to you in such a way that you will not be able to see it any other way. Spirit will sometimes put people in your path who carry particular messages, and they will come at just the right time. This story illustrates that.

The alignment of all the things that had to happen to bring this story to you still boggles my mind. When you are in service to Spirit and people, sometimes things align, and you will not believe in coincidences any longer.

It happened in a place I certainly never expected: Costco.

It was a warm fall afternoon when I ventured into Costco. I was in a bit of a hurry and needed only a few things. As I stood in line, waiting to pay, I realized that I was hungry, so I went for a hot dog in the store.

A young man with two young children was standing in front of me. He kept turning around, looking at me, before finally saying, "You're Shawn Leonard."

I didn't recognize him, so I had to ask how we met.

"We didn't actually meet, but I came to your show in Halifax—at the Forum."

I rarely recall the specifics of any readings I do as it's just way too much information to keep in my head, so I asked if I read him.

"Well, you tried," he said and chuckled, "but I don't think I was ready. You came to my side of the stage and pointed to the area where I was sitting. You said there was a mother figure named Mildred who was trying to make a connection, but I didn't own it."

"Was that your mom's name?"

"It was; I just wasn't ready. That night really opened my eyes, though." The man's food arrived.

"I'm glad," I said. "She was trying to get your attention. Thanks for letting me know. Enjoy your lunch."

I assumed that was the end of our interaction, but a few minutes later I was standing, hands still full of groceries but now with a soft drink and hot dog, looking for a place to sit. Wouldn't you know, but the only free table in the entire seating area was with the young man and his two young kids.

I walked over and asked if I could sit with them. He agreed and introduced himself as Dan Glover.

"You know, it's kind of funny I'm running into you today," he said.

I knew something was up. When the only seat in the food court was next to Dan, I figured there was a reason for our meeting. It didn't take long to figure out what was going on. "Why's that?" I asked.

"Well, I'm pretty sure it was my mom who was trying to communicate with you at your show. I just wasn't ready then. Now today is her birthday, and here I am running into you. Seems like a bit of a coincidence."

"Well, there are no coincidences." I smiled at him as I began to feel his mother very much around us, trying to get my attention. I was pretty sure she had arranged for us to meet here at Costco. Then I got a very specific piece of information: "Your mom wants you to know you don't need to put anything on her grave. You can just plant something, or have flowers at your house, and she can enjoy them there. She's always with you."

His face blanched. "What did you just say?"

"She doesn't need you to plant anything on her grave."

"How did you know that?" Dan had stopped eating now.

"Your mother is letting me know," I said. "She's right here with you."

"I just planted a blue juniper on her grave, like two days ago," he said. "And when I walked in here today there were five or six employees planting blue junipers outside. I thought it was a bit strange, so I called my wife to tell her." Dan shook his head. "And now you're telling me my mom's right here?"

"That's right," I said, and quickly other information became apparent; I saw his mother had died in a fire.

"Your mom died in a fire when you were young. She was young too. Yet, she wasn't alone; I can see she was with her sister?"

Dan nodded quietly, agreeing with everything I said. I could practically see the goose bumps erupting on his body.

"She almost got out of the house."

"She did?" Dan hadn't known that piece of information, but later confirmed with an uncle that his mother's body had been found just inside the doorway. Dan was only 10 at the time and had been out with his father when his mother and his aunt had accidentally set the house on fire. They both perished, but I could see they hadn't suffered.

"Your mom passed out from smoke inhalation," I said. "She was unconscious. She didn't suffer." Suddenly, I felt someone touching my left shoulder. I knew it was Dan's mother, trying to direct my attention to something on her son's left shoulder. I could see it then in my mind's eye: a tattoo! He had a tattoo of his mother's face. Dan had on three-quarter-length sleeves, so I couldn't see the tattoo but knew it was there. "She wants you to know she's pretty impressed with that artwork you've got on your shoulder," I said, pointing to where I knew it was. Dan's entire face crumpled as he broke down, crying hard.

Tears streamed down his face as he raised his sleeve up over his shoulder to show me his mother's face.

"None of this was an accident, us meeting today," I said. "Your mom orchestrated all of this. It's her birthday, and we were meant to share this moment so I could give you this message: she loves you, and she knows who your children are. She's very proud of you."

Mildred Glover would have been 50 the day I ran into her son at Costco. What happened to her was a tragedy for the family. While none of us can possibly understand the timing of a loved one's death, I do know there's always a reason for everything. I felt so humbled Mildred had chosen me to deliver her important message to her son. I was so happy she was able to give Dan such solid reassurance. After that day at Costco he knew, without a shadow of a doubt, his mom was always with him and always had been—terrifically proud, and loving him fiercely.

CHAPTER 15

Ila'kwenawete'wk Mimajuinuikultijik

GUIDES IN PHYSICAL FORM

When you pay attention and you go with the flow of where life wants to take you, it's easy to see our existence here on Earth as one *hello* and one *good-bye* after another—and I'm not just talking about death! I'm also referring to the way our situation changes over time when we listen to our own inner guide and allow ourselves to be directed. We humans seldom stay in the same place for long, energetically speaking, and if we do we quickly become stagnant.

In my own life, I have found this to be true for the people I surround myself with. Shortly after my divorce, a member of the paranormal group was trying to insert herself into my life, and everything about her raised a huge red flag. I left the group but took the extra step of asking my guides to kindly do whatever they needed to make sure I didn't ever run into that person again.

They came through on their promise, in a way I never could have anticipated. It happened on a day I was downtown delivering the mail. It was early morning and not many people were up and about. In fact, none of the stores were even open except one: a newspaper, magazine, coffee shop.

I walked up a hill on my route, almost colliding with a very tall man and a quite short woman who were coming around the corner at that exact moment. The tall man got right in my face. He looked familiar in a way I couldn't immediately place.

"I'm not from around here," the tall man said. "My name is Sam, and I'm looking for a place to go eat breakfast."

What the heck? What was the likelihood, on a quiet, early morning, of being approached and chatted up by two separate people within minutes of each other? When I normally walked this route I didn't see a soul.

"Can you tell me a good place to eat breakfast?" he repeated. Remember the *Seinfeld* episode with the close talker? That was this guy. He was definitely in my physical space, and every time I tried to inch backward, he and his companion crept forward. I stole a glance at her; she looked concerned. Breakfast? I began to think about places that might be open so early. There was the Bluenose II down on Barrington Street, and . . .

The man interrupted my thoughts. "Well, I know the Bluenose II is just down the hill," he said.

I thought he said he wasn't from here? Did he actually say his name was Sam? Why introduce himself just to ask me directions? That felt weird, so I turned my thoughts back to breakfast. There was also Smitty's, up on Spring Garden Road across from the public gardens. As soon as I thought this, he again chimed in.

"And then there's Smitty's, up near the public gardens."

I was beginning to feel the goose bumps that come when something unusual, and a little other-worldly, happens. I blurted out, "I thought you weren't from around here?"

Sam leaned in even closer, and said with a smile, "You know what? It's okay. I know where we are going."

And then they walked around me! *What a strange interaction,* I thought. The person whom I had asked for protection from was right in front of me, turning to head uphill and walking the other way. I turned on my heel and did a 180-degree turn. To my astonishment everyone I had just been talking to, and who had walked past me, had completely vanished! The tall man and his concerned companion were gone. They had completely disappeared. I shook my head. They had just been here; literally only seconds had passed.

In that moment I put all the pieces together. I suddenly knew Sam and Victoria had actually taken physical form to help me avoid the person who I intuitively felt wanted to cause me trouble. Sam had even named himself, which explained why he looked familiar! I realized they were delaying me. Had they not, I would have likely run right into the woman from my paranormal group. They were helping me, doing what I asked them to.

After, I replayed the situation in my mind hundreds of times, wanting to understand the timing. Why then and not another time? Did they know something I didn't about what may have happened had I run into that person?

I remain immensely grateful for my brief encounter with them in physical form, and their intervention. I would love for my guides to appear to me in human bodies in the future, and have asked for the awareness to really appreciate the next time it happens.

The lesson here is to not underestimate the ability of your guides to intercede if need be. Guides can and will help you one way or another, especially if you have regular dialogue telling them out loud what you need help with. If they can appear for me, they can possibly appear for you. Speak to your guides like they are a trusted friend who has your back, always.

CHAPTER 16

KITPUEY PI'KUN M'PISUN

EAGLE FEATHER MEDICINE

One of the joys of being back in Nova Scotia was immersing myself in the beautiful landscape where I grew up. Along with a few old friends, I started an annual tradition of kayaking down the Shubenacadie River, from Enfield to Elmsdale. One year, not long after my experience of being aided by the Indigenous Elder in spirit form on McNabs Island, my friends and I were out for our kayak down the river. It was a beautiful day, and as I drifted out ahead of the rest, I noticed an eagle sitting in a tree. It looked young, and I intuitively felt it was a female.

She watched as I kayaked by. I was maybe three or four hundred feet past when suddenly she flew right over my head. I heard her before I saw her, and goose bumps erupted over my entire body as I watched her land very close by in another tree. She continued to watch me, and then did the same thing again; she waited until I had passed before sweeping right over the top of the kayak and landing in another tree.

Since my encounter with the spirit on McNabs Island I'd done a little reading about proper smudging and knew the process involved an eagle feather. I had also found out these feathers must be given to the person who uses them. This eagle's close proximity, as well as the sense she was watching and following me, made me wonder if an eagle feather was coming to me that day.

With this in mind, I spoke to her as she flew over me for the third and fourth time. "Kitpu," (pronounced Git-pu) I said out loud, voice raised. It was the Mi'kmaq word for eagle. "I would appreciate an eagle feather. I've been looking for one, but haven't found any. Is there a way you could give me one? I could use your spiritual medicine for the work I do."

Nothing happened. I was still ahead of the others, and as I paddled farther down the river, she did it again. And again. And again. Each time she flew so close to my head I could feel her wings graze my hair. Finally, after about the tenth swoop over the top of me and my boat, a feather dropped from the sky and landed in the water. I raced like crazy to get it.

She was watching from a nearby tree as I finally reached into the water and fished it out. There was a little crick in it with a piece missing. I had been hoping for a large, magnificent eagle feather, but what I got was a smaller, not-so-perfect one. Do you know what I had the nerve to say? I looked up at her and asked, "Do you have a better feather?" She had stayed steadfastly with me all the way down the river, but when I uttered that question, she took one look at me and flew off. I didn't see her again for the rest of the day. At the time I didn't really know much about Native culture, so I didn't know that I should have thanked the eagle in Mi'kmaq. I should have said, "Wela'lin, Kitpu, for your gift and spiritual medicine. I will honor your trust in me."

Since then, I've learned so much about my Indigenous tradition. I've learned the eagle is sacred because it flies the highest, and therefore comes closest to the Creator. In the Mi'kmaq creation story, the eagle flies above all the storms, and all the negativity and darkness of the world. When an eagle descends to earth to help you, and gifts you its spiritual medicine with a feather, it's a high honor. I have since gone back to the river and placed Tobacco in the water and spoke words of gratitude and thanks.

Despite having received many other eagle feathers since then, this first one is still very special to me. I honor it and know it was meant for me. I am so grateful for each feather gifted during my life, and eagle medicine continues to help me clear and move energy with people who need it.

If you are meant to work with eagle medicine, I believe an eagle feather will come to you. Talk to our Source, our Creator, even to the eagles themselves, and ask for a feather. Eagle medicine can help us all through our darkest times. If you use eagle medicine to help others heal, or clear their energy, it is a great gift indeed.

Not all people are meant to work with eagle medicine or meant to have an eagle feather and that is okay; work with the medicine that Spirit gifts you.

The raven, the hawk, the owl, and many other birds and animals also carry medicine.

Work with the medicine that comes to you, and honor that with your full heart.

MEDITATION FOR WORKING
WITH EAGLE MEDICINE

Please sit or lie in a comfortable space and location, where you will not be disturbed.

Ask the Creator and Ancestors to surround you with an unconditional loving light of divine guidance and protection.

Close your eyes and take three slow deep breaths.

Now envision yourself with your psychic inner eyes, standing beside a riverbank.

As you watch the water flow downstream, you notice an eagle soaring, gliding back and forth high over your head.

You see a large tree with one limb that hangs over the other side of the river, very near you.

The eagle perches upon that limb and intently stares deep into your eyes.

You can sense the spiritual wisdom and energetic medicine the eagle contains.

In the blink of an eye, you and the eagle are one, and you become the Eagle.

You take flight and can see all the trees and the long, winding river.

You notice and see all things with clarity and have the ability to hyper focus upon whatever you choose.

The eagle lands where you stood, and you and the Eagle are one.

If there is an issue in your life that needs to be addressed, ask the eagle spirit to help you see the best direction for you with its clear vision.

If facing this situation causes you stress, fear, or even anxiety, feel the eagle's large wingspan fanning over your spirit and aura as you now stand at the riverbank.

In doing so, your spirit and aura are cleared.

Watch the eagle fly high, back up into the sky until it vanishes into the sun itself.

Allow the sunlight to recharge you and illuminate your spirit and aura allowing no darkness, fear, or stress to remain.

Now open your eyes and go through life in a good way.

Carry clear insight, allowing Eagle Medicine to guide you always.

CHAPTER 17

MESKI'K
KET+MOQJETESKAWEK
THE BIG NUDGE

Spirit has a way of guiding us through life and pushing us toward where we are meant to be. We get in our own way sometimes, whether we continue with unhealthy patterns because it feels easier, or by staying in situations that don't always serve us because we're afraid of the repercussions. Sometimes we can be shortsighted in our own lives. I have realized that Spirit has a plan for all of us, and if we feel a nudge to make a change and shift our lives, it's because there is a divine design to the universe and our world.

I recognize this within my own life, and a good example of how Spirit can push you to where you need to be rather than where you *think* you need to be happened after I relocated to Nova Scotia. I was booking clients six months in advance, and I started to do about a dozen readings per week and began organizing public live shows. Despite the success of being able to start from scratch in a new place, and that clients were finding me without me having to advertise, I felt compelled to hang on to my Canada Post job because it was a reliable income, with benefits and a pension.

I felt called to become a full-time psychic medium, and I didn't fully trust that I could make it work at first. My guides were patient with me, and I was continually reminded of what my real calling was and had received several reinforcing messages that it was safe to leave my nine-to-five job. Yet I simply couldn't rationalize doing it; the fear of not having enough money to pay my bills, living expenses, and child and spousal support paralyzed me.

I continued to ignore these messages to the point that Spirit had to step in with a stronger nudge, and it was one I wouldn't be able to ignore. The fear that had paralyzed me mentally from making that change in my life now began to have real-life implications, and as a result my body broke down and began to paralyze me physically. It took major physical hardship for me to learn it's easier to just let go and trust, and I'm telling you this story with the hope you will not let fear control your life or your choices, because the reality is all our choices in life have an impact whether we realize they do or not.

It started with a tear in my meniscus in my left knee, which led to multiple knee surgeries. As I was trying to heal, I herniated the L3-L4 disc in my back, which was excruciatingly painful, and I had to use a wheelchair and was unable to work at all for a time. I was placed on a long waiting list for back surgery and was prescribed strong painkillers, and as a result I ended up having to temporarily suspend all my readings. It was a dark time in my life. I went to chiropractors, laser therapy, physiotherapy, and acupuncture. I thought I was doing everything I could, but for a while it felt like nothing helped.

Slowly, I started to heal, and although I was still reliant on a wheelchair, I was able to do readings again. More importantly, I had developed a new sense of clarity, and I realized these physical challenges were serving as the big nudge that I needed to make some necessary changes in my life.

As a result, I developed a new inner strength, as well as an increased psychic connection during this time. It was apparent that my ability to connect was even more accurate and tuned in when I wasn't exhausted from working a physically demanding full-time job. Even as I made the decision to quit, I still had a lot of fear attached to that decision, but I also felt enormously supported by the universe—and relieved that I had finally done it.

Everything came together and continued to flow, and as I grew physically stronger each day, and healed more and more, I was able to do even more readings and events without the distraction of another job.

Letting go of our fears can be very difficult, but it's necessary for growth. Often it can feel easier to continue doing what we have grown accustomed to, rather than shift our perspectives in a way that better serves us. We can get in our own way most of the time and feel weighed down by responsibilities others place on us, and those we place on ourselves.

It's therefore important to trust when we feel nudged by Spirit to make those decisions, because Spirit has a plan for us that we are not always privy to.

Being a spirit talker is part of my mission, and there was a reason for that dark period in my life. Had I not been pushed more deeply into that role, I likely wouldn't have been able to serve as many people as I have been so fortunate to. There have been moments in my life that divine intervention has taken place, where I felt Spirit led me to a certain path. This is likely the case for most of you, that you have been faced with seemingly endless roadblocks in a situation or, on the flip side, you have been pushed into leaving something behind only to realize it wasn't meant for you in the first place.

Sometimes we need to have faith that our guides, angels, Ancestors, and the Creator have a plan for us. We just need to quiet our minds for a moment and realize that we are safe, and we are protected. If you have felt a calling within your own life, trust that the universe will collaborate with you and help guide you to the right people and circumstances to make that dream a reality.

AFFIRMATIONS FOR TRUSTING IN SPIRIT

Speak these affirmations out loud, and from your heart center:

I am divinely supported and loved in all experiences of life.

I know bad things happen to direct me to where I am supposed to be.

I trust my divine purpose and spirit guides, even through times when I struggle.

I surrender fear and embrace my purpose.

CHAPTER 18

KISIKU NEYA'SIT

AN ELDER APPEARS

As I developed and grew as a medium, and became better known in Nova Scotia, there came opportunities to donate my services to worthwhile causes. In 2013, Veith House, a nonprofit organization in Halifax, asked me to give a free evening of readings. I was happy to do it, and certainly had no idea how significantly my life would change afterward.

The audience was small enough—about 50 people— for me to connect with almost everybody in the room, even if only for a short time. There was a Mi'kmaq woman sitting in the front row with another, younger woman, who looked as though she might be her daughter. When I connected with the older woman an important piece of information was immediately delivered by me to her.

"The spirit world is telling me very clearly, you've recently heard about four Indigenous people who were missing, murdered I believe, in the Cape Breton area. I see a large body of water, perhaps the Bras d'Or Lake area, and a hill leading up from the water. I feel there is a person named Joe connected to the story. If you figure out who Joe is, tell him I know where their remains are. Do you know anything about this?"

She and her daughter exchanged a quick look. "I just learned of this story yesterday," the older woman said. "I met with someone who told me about it."

The information was coming fast, and I knew it was important. "I have a feeling you're a writer, or some kind of storyteller, and there is a calling for you to somehow put this story out there."

She thanked me and I moved on, but after the night ended the two women stayed in my mind. Up to that point I hadn't had much opportunity to read people from my own culture. In fact, that event marked the first time I had ever connected so strongly with somebody who was also Mi'kmaq. I had a feeling the Great Spirit was in the midst of answering a prayer I had put out there after my experience on McNabs Island, when the Indigenous Elder from the spirit world had appeared. This encounter made me hunger for a connection with a living Mi'kmaq Elder; one who could teach me more about Indigenous cultural and spiritual traditions.

Sure enough, the woman from the night at Veith House contacted me privately. We became friends and, over time, I told her I was looking for a mentor. She told me there was someone I should meet, and before I knew it a Mi'kmaq Elder was standing on my doorstep, holding something in his arms. I was soon to learn he was carrying what is called a bundle, which contained a sacred eagle wing along with the traditional medicines of Sage, Sweetgrass, Tobacco, and Cedar.

"I heard you want to learn about traditional ways," he said.

I invited him in and offered him a cup of tea. We settled in my office, where I did client readings, for our chat. I told him that although I was Mi'kmaq, I hadn't been raised with traditional practices. The Elder placed the bundle on the table and unwrapped it. The first thing I noticed was the enormous eagle wing, stitched with very fine beadwork.

"I see you have some feathers." He pointed to ones that adorned my office. I noticed the Elder chose his words carefully, and never said more than what was required. He went on to tell me feathers were gifts from the Great Spirit, and taught me how to respect these gifts by handling them in the right way. During that first visit he also showed me how to do proper smudging, in addition to teaching me some Mi'kmaq words. As he left, he invited me to be part of a couple of upcoming events, including a sweat lodge ceremony.

As the Elder continued to teach me in the traditional ways and expose me to Mi'kmaq culture, he came to a few of my events and saw the work I was doing. He came to believe in my ability to connect to the spirit world, and even said he saw me as a spiritual healer.

As we worked together, it became clear the murdered Indigenous people I felt in the reading at Veith House were the Elder's relatives. I tentatively broached the subject one day and asked if he was interested in hearing what information I was being sent via the spirit world. He was open to the experience, and I was able to provide some details about how his relatives had died, and at whose hands. I further asked if he would like my help locating their bodies, as I already had a feeling I knew where they were.

He accepted my offer of help and together with my friend Doug, who owns a cadaver dog, we traveled to Big Pond, Cape Breton, in Nova Scotia. We searched the area where I felt his relatives' bodies were buried, and Doug's dog, Breya, indicated an area under a tree, which was probably over 50 years old. Doug had brought another friend who owned a search-and-rescue dog, and her dog also indicated the same location. I felt satisfied knowing I may have given the Elder some sort of closure with my information, as well as the location of his relatives' bodies. This felt like my way of thanking him for his teachings.

We shared many special moments over the years he served as a teacher and guide. One of my proudest moments came when the Elder gave me my Mi'kmaq name: Wape'k Kitpu Aknutmajik Jijaqmijk, which means White Eagle Spirit Talker. During the year that preceded the gift of my name, I had found three, pure-white eagle tail feathers. I don't think this was an accident; it felt like everything was coming together.

Later, the Elder gifted me with a walking stick upon which my new Mi'kmaq name was written. Yet perhaps the biggest honor he bestowed upon me was the gift of his eagle wing, which I had seen on the day of our very first visit. It had been given to him by an Elder who had taught him many years before, and tradition dictated he pass this wing on to a student when a new wing entered his life. This had just happened; the Elder had been gifted a new wing from a local wildlife park and decided I would be the recipient of the one he had carried for years.

He told me I should use this wing to heal people and clear their energy. Then he taught me how to properly smudge with smoke using this sacred object and spiritual plant medicines like White Buffalo Sage, Cedar, and

Sweetgrass. He also instructed I keep it wrapped inside the bundle, which was made of a red cloth, to keep it protected and clear from outside energies.

I felt very honored by this sacred gift and carry it with me when I travel for events, using the wing to smudge the room where everyone will gather. I also use it during any of my sessions where a client may be going through a particularly hard time. I know smudging them with the wing will help them move, or release, some of the energy they're carrying.

Someday, when I become an Elder and share the teachings, and when a new wing comes into my life, I will pass this eagle wing to another student on their journey.

CHAPTER 19

TETPAQTA'SIK AQ PUJITE'TASIK

VALIDATION AND TRUST

When people come to see a medium, often what they're looking for is evidence their loved one still exists, and may be hoping some contact can be established. The validation aspect of a session should be taken very, very seriously. I have become known for the accuracy of the information I give, especially names. Not all mediums receive names from the spirit world, so I consider myself to be very attuned to clairaudience, which is the ability to hear spirit messages. Sometimes I hear names quite clearly, and other times I receive images that help paint a picture.

Such was the case with a young woman who came to see me, looking to connect with her grandmother. This happened quickly and easily, and I was able to give the young woman all kinds of specific information, including how and when her grandmother died. Yet I could tell the woman was waiting for something else, something very specific. Just then, an unusual image popped into my mind, one I'd not seen before. It was a glass of milk and a saucer with three cookies.

"I have to ask you something. Your grandma is showing me milk and cookies on a plate. Does that mean anything to you?"

The young woman replied no, she didn't know what the image meant. I tried to move on, but it was like the grandmother wouldn't let me. She kept repeating the same image: milk and cookies, milk and cookies, over and over in my mind's eye.

"Are you sure?" I asked again. "She keeps reiterating milk and cookies, and she's not giving up. She's being very insistent."

All of a sudden, the young woman sat right up and shouted, "Oh my God! Cookie! You got it!"

"Sorry?" Although my client seemed very happy by what had just happened, I was still mystified.

"Before I came today, I asked my grandma to send her nickname because it's something no one else knows. Her nickname was Cookie! Now I *know* it's her."

For me, this was an excellent example of having to trust what appears, and also a reminder to be patient while the client catches up with their relative in the spirit world. The grandmother knew her granddaughter needed to hear the word "cookie," and she did her best to get me to say it repeatedly!

Validation can also come in the form of memories or experiences, which no one else but the person sitting in front of me and their deceased loved one could possibly know. One of the most startling examples of this occurred a few years ago. Jessica was a young 17-year-old who passed away suddenly from an undiagnosed heart condition. Her parents made an appointment and Jessica began communicating with me in earnest, telling me information about her passing, asking me to tell her parents she was okay and she loved them. It was then that something very unusual happened, something I never expected to experience. Jessica gave me an image of herself in a bra. This was very awkward. I make a point of trusting everything I receive from Spirit and voicing what I see, even if I don't understand. This, however, seemed terribly inappropriate. How do you tell two grieving parents their daughter just showed up in only a bra? I took a deep breath and began by apologizing.

"I want you to know how sorry I am about your daughter's passing." I paused and cleared my throat. "Sometimes people who have passed will show me unexpected things. Your daughter is showing me something that feels awkward, but I trust it's for a reason and you will understand, even if I don't."

They looked at me expectantly.

"Your daughter is appearing to me in only a bra." I felt terribly embarrassed and could feel my face turning red. "I can see she is quite large-chested, and there is something strangely very significant about the bra I am supposed to talk to you about."

Imagine my relief when their jaws nearly hit the floor and they began laughing. But their laughter soon turned to tears as the reality of their daughter's presence was vividly confirmed. "It's her. It's definitely her," they said, nodding vigorously and clutching each other's hands. They went on to tell me how their daughter had often been teased for her chest, especially by her sister, who called her "big boobs." On the first anniversary of Jessica's passing, the family got everyone together to celebrate Jessica's life and honor her memory. They bedazzled one of Jessica's bras, decorating it with all things bright and sparkling.

This is why it had been important for Jessica to show me her bra. It was a piece of unique information no one but close family and friends knew. This isn't something you would post on Facebook. This isn't something you would write on a blog. This was the thing Jessica knew would allow her parents to believe she was still there and still with them, just no longer in physical form.

The last story I will share in this chapter is also a very unique one. A woman who hadn't booked under her own name, and who seemed quite suspicious, had come to see me. She didn't tell me with whom she was trying to connect, but someone came through right away. It was a young man who I felt had taken his own life. I sensed he had been her boyfriend. He apologized to her for what had happened, and told her it wasn't her fault. He talked about having been depressed and on drugs, and encouraged her to find her way in life. He said although he hadn't been mentally well in life, he was healthy and happy in the spirit world and had finally found peace. He then showed me an image of himself onstage with a microphone, looking vibrant and healthy. Suddenly, a guy walked out from behind him. It was Tupac Shakur, the famous rapper who had also passed away. The guy put his arm around Tupac, and there they stood together in front of the mic.

"I'm not sure why I'm getting this, but your boyfriend is showing me an image of himself on a stage with Tupac Shakur. Do you know who he is?"

"Oh my God! Are you kidding me?!" she yelled, jumping up off the couch. She then yanked off her hoodie and hauled up the back of her T-shirt. Covering her entire back was an enormous tattoo of Tupac Shakur. "My boyfriend and I both loved Tupac, so we got matching tattoos. He had the exact same one on his back."

She went on to tell me she had thought the whole medium thing was not real or possible. That is why she hadn't booked under her real name, so I couldn't find out any information before our session. "There is no way you could have known about my boyfriend or Tupac," she said. "And I know you didn't see my tattoo because I was wearing a hoodie the whole time." Suddenly, the reality of knowing her boyfriend was right there, communicating with her, overwhelmed her and she broke down in tears. "It's really him. Tell him I love him. I still love him so much."

"And he loves you," I assured.

I guess that puts to rest the theory that Tupac is still alive. He is very much alive—in the spirit world.

These three stories are just a small sampling of the amazing ways in which the spirit communicates. Some days I can hardly believe I am lucky enough to have been given this ability to act as a bridge between this and the spirit world. Being able to provide this kind of comfort, as well as being able to help heal grieving hearts, is a true gift.

You, too, have the power to connect with people you care about and miss dearly in the spirit world. Importantly, we all have memories that just pop into our minds out of the blue. Often, people believe their thoughts are just that: thoughts. Imagine, the moment you think of someone in the spirit world, they know you are thinking of them— especially during those moments where you reflect and remember a specific time together.

So, from this day forward, please do yourself and the people in the light you care about a favor: acknowledge out loud, or in your mind, that you know they are with you. Open your mind, heart, and spirit, and feel them within and surrounding you. Feel the love you share for each other in that moment. Thank them!

Many people feel alone, but if you only knew who walks with you along your journey, you would never feel alone again. All your people and all your animals in the spirit world are only a thought away.

CHAPTER 20

Mu'eskmatasinuk Nutasin

AN UNEXPECTED VOICE

There is all kinds of guidance available to us at all times—it's just that very few of us know how to access it, while others (like me) can be quite good at ignoring it. Our guides communicate with us in so many ways: through our intuition, our feelings, or our gut sense something is off or wrong. We always have the choice whether or not to listen, but our guides are always on our side.

Throughout my life I've also felt the guiding hand of my father, and occasionally have felt the presence of someone who was well known during their time on Earth, both of whom have passed on. Perhaps the most unexpected, and special, was with Jesus. I'm quite aware writing these words may alienate some readers, but I'm willing to do so because I feel it's important everyone reading this understand there are many sources of wisdom available to each and every one of us.

Let me first let you know where I am coming from. I personally don't consider the Bible to be the word of God, and I don't believe in the Biblical Jesus. Rather, I believe in a much different, all-loving teacher and healer who was put on the earth to help us. I believe Jesus was a very real human being who healed people, who died for his beliefs, and who was willing to do all that because he knew no matter what happened both he and his message would live on. He was a deeply spiritual person who understood, and used, his connection to the Creator or God or the Great Spirit (or whichever word you want to use for the infinite energy of love). It's the same connection to which we all have access—but most of us don't know this.

My encounter with Jesus happened one morning as I was lying in bed after a hurtful incident the night before. My children were not thrilled that I had a new partner at the time, and I had sent them an e-mail explaining my stance. I was struggling emotionally. I was terribly worried that I would not be able to mend this issue with my children. I also didn't want my children to dislike my partner, or ruin the possibility of them having a relationship with her.

I was unable to sleep and could hear my guides trying to insert themselves in my thoughts, but I wasn't open to listening. Just then, a loud voice within my mind sounded clear. "Shun." It was just this one word, which I recognized as my name laced with a distinct Hebrew accent.

I don't hear loud voices very often, so it took me by surprise. I lay in stunned silence. A minute later, the voice repeated my name. "Shun!"

This time I answered. "Yes?" I immediately heard this message, loud and clear: "Shun, you do not have a bad family; you have a good family."

I had never heard another voice like it, before or since, and I had never felt so much love and compassion from any other spirit voice. Even today, when I think of the sound of the voice and what he said, it's easy for me to well up with emotion.

When I heard that voice, I knew that my guides had gotten the man known as Jesus to talk to me, as I wasn't listening to them and they understood I was really struggling. The one simple sentence he shared, delivered with so much love, compassion, and wisdom, changed me. And it changed how I felt. It enabled me to know somehow, with time, all would work itself out. And it did.

Having heard the voice on that particular day made me wish I had heard it sooner. Hearing that one sentence taught me so much: I know he's there and I know he's a connection point to the Creator—in the same way as my guides. He is an ascended master with great wisdom, compassion, and knowledge of the heart.

After, I remembered conversations Sam and I would have when I was a kid. I remember things he said about who Jesus really was, and I had another look at my notes from my days with the Novus Spiritus Church. I read with interest that Jesus was likely not his actual name. It was likely Joshua, which in Aramaic and Hebrew would have been pronounced "Yeshua."

This experience cemented my belief that the Creator is within all of us. It's a connection we all carry inside our hearts. I encourage you to trust any loving voices that come through. That infinite, divine love is there for all of us, at any time. We just need an open heart—and open mind—to hear it.

RECEIVING MESSAGES

There are two things you can do to receive a message from the spirit world. The first and most important aspect is your prayerful words and affirmations. When you speak with the spirit world, speak clearly and from your heart. I have included a few affirmations below you can use, or if you choose to speak your own loving affirmative words, that is equally as good. Speak them out loud and from your heart center.

I accept help from the ascended masters.

I am worthy to hear spirit guidance from all beings in the light.

I accept the unconditional loving words that Spirit will speak to me.

The second aspect of receiving guidance from the spirit world or an ascended master is creating space. In the above story I was resting in bed and was working at mindfulness. It is in the mind that is not full of thoughts where you create space to hear. Meditate and be mindful, focusing on your breath. Just be and breathe . . . Remember, *this too shall pass.* It always does.

CHAPTER 21

WELTESKUJ KAPLI'EL
MEETING GABRIEL

I wanted to visit Charlottetown, Prince Edward Island, for a self-produced event at the Rodd Charlottetown Hotel. I loved this venue because of its history; it was built in 1931 by the Canadian National Railway. It was a smaller venue, and a very intimate experience. The event went well, with roughly 90 percent of the audience staying after for pictures and to ask questions. I felt very happy being able to validate the spirit messages I was being sent.

After everybody left, I gathered all my sound equipment and personal belongings and walked out of the room. I noticed a dime on the floor, which quickly grabbed my attention. The strange thing was I had just walked right by and had not seen it. I felt my father was with me, and I acknowledged it—feeling as though he attended my event that evening and was proud of me. With a smile I put the dime in my pocket.

Feeling tired and grateful, my partner and I headed to our room on the fifth floor. We had not been there until now, and she went in before me as I was pushing our luggage through the doorway. I had left one suitcase just outside the door, and I wanted to grab it as quickly as I could. When I opened the door, I was surprised to see a five-dollar bill sitting perfectly flat on top of the suitcase. I grabbed it and placed it in my pocket, scanning up and down the hall for other people. *Strange*, I thought to myself. *Perhaps my dad is trying to tell me something.*

I quickly fell asleep and slipped into a dark dream I've had several times. The dream is typically dark and fearful. There is a cloaked older woman in the room where I lay awake in my dream, and she is holding me down on the bed. I try to push her off me, feeling as though she is sitting on my chest, sucking out my life energy. It always ends in the same way: I am trying to push her off until I finally relax and surround myself with light, which I blow into her face. She immediately dissipates. I wake up still blowing air out of my mouth, frightened, until I realize it was just a dream. I have had this dream for about 20 years.

At 3 A.M. I instantly jumped up out of bed and began to pace the room, thinking about my dad visiting and leaving me signs. I decided to smudge myself and the room. I prayed and spoke to the Great Spirit, my guides, and my father to not allow the dream to once again occur after I fall asleep.

I've had readings with people who describe similar dreams. I've also read extensively about this dream experience and have discovered many people have an issue with sleep paralysis. In Newfoundland, my Mi'kmaq grandmother called this dark spirit the Old Hag. My guides have explained she isn't negative at all, but is rather a spirit whose sole purpose is to make sure our own spirits don't get stuck in the astral-realm world while we're in this in-between state. Our spirit body gets pushed back into our physical body if we wake before our spirit returns. Hence, seeing and feeling as if that Old Hag were sitting on my chest, holding me down.

My guides have told me to allow them to help facilitate a clean exit, and entrance, back into my body from the dream and astral world. I hastened to do this after this last experience and quickly fell back to sleep. My next dream was different. I began to see and feel myself surrounded by light. In the room was a man around 30 years old, wearing a long white robe, and with short, black curly hair. As he walked up to me he seemed radiant, glowing with light.

"Shawn," he said. "Do not fear me, Shawn!"

"Do not fear you! Why would I fear you?"

"Shawn, I want you to know you will soon be going through a very difficult and dark time. I want you to know I am going to be with you and will help protect you through it all."

"Who are you?" I asked. "Are you a new spirit guide? I do not recognize you."

"My name is Gabriel," he replied. "I am like a spirit guide, but I am not. Remember, I am with you and will help you."

I woke up at 7 A.M. and explained to my partner the new dream I had, asking what she thought it meant. She didn't know. I called a Mi'kmaq Elder on our way back to Nova Scotia. I wanted to see if he could meet me and discuss the dreams and sequence of events.

He was alarmed when I told him everything, and explained Gabriel was an angel, a messenger from the Creator and the Great Spirit. The Elder believed Gabriel had been sent to me in preparation for something negative that was about to disrupt my life. I was surprised I met the angel Gabriel, although confused as to why I didn't know he was an angel. I didn't see any wings! I have never seen, nor met, an angel of light before, yet I knew he was wise, loving, and compassionate, and made me feel I would be safe during whatever was coming. The Elder told me to pray, meditate, and smudge regularly, and said he would do pipe ceremonies as soon as he could.

One month after the event in Prince Edward Island and the dreams, my current relationship ended. It is natural: people come into your life for a season, a reason, or sometimes a lifetime.

While I knew Gabriel was supporting me, I needed further guidance and called a dear friend and soul sister, Anne Bérubé.

REMEMBERING YOUR DREAMS

Many people struggle to remember their dreams, as they contain important information about your past, present, and potential future. One tip I give is to talk to your guides out loud and ask that they help you remember your dreams by waking you when you are at the latter part of a rapid eye movement (REM) cycle. This is typically when you are in the dreamworld having the experiences that you do.

A dream catcher has been used by many Indigenous cultures as a device to help protect people from bad dreams. Typically, the dream catcher is placed inside a window in your bedroom. The bad dreams are caught in the web of the catcher and the good ones are allowed through. We are all creators and when you give power to a thought like this it may serve its purpose. Although I have a different idea in relation to a dream catcher. I use mine as a trigger object! I have placed a dream catcher in a specific spot in my bedroom where I see it upon waking. I immediately look for the dream catcher as a trigger object to help remind me what I just dreamed about.

Finally, consider keeping a dream journal beside your bedroom nightstand along with a handy pen or pencil to jot down immediate thoughts in relation to the dreams you've just had. Upon fully waking read what you have jotted down in your journal. This will help with dream recall and analyzation. This way you can reflect on the deeper meaning as to what your dreams are revealing to you.

CHAPTER 22

KLUJJEWTA'SIKEWE'L AQ WELA'SUWAQN

BLESSINGS AND GRATITUDE

Guidance doesn't come only from the spirit world; it can also come through people who are put in your path and are very much alive in the physical world. The Elder who taught me so much, and propelled me further down my spiritual path, is an example of someone living who played a huge role in my growth. That Elder, unbeknownst to him, also reintroduced me to someone else who would become hugely important.

Anne Bérubé has played a big role as I've learned to trust myself in both my relationships and my profession.

We first met when she came to me for a reading many years ago, but we crossed paths again years later at a Mi'kmaq ceremonial healing and talking circle.

The minute I saw Anne I knew our meeting again wasn't an accident. In fact, she was in the midst of producing an event for another psychic and asked if I wanted to come as her guest. I didn't know it at the time, but Anne and her company, Autopoetic Ideas, had been responsible for bringing James Van Praagh, Anita Moorjani, Deepak Chopra, and Wayne Dyer to the Maritimes. As we got to know each other, it became a bit of a no-brainer we would also work together in the future. Anne, a Hay House author and spiritual coach, travels around the world speaking about embodied spirituality. The messages we share very much complement each other, so Anne and I began planning and speaking at events together. Over time, I learned one of Anne's early mentors was the late Wayne Dyer. The two had been close friends as well as business associates, and Anne missed him terribly. On one occasion she even asked if I could connect with him. It wasn't hard; he came through with a clear message, appearing for her as a butterfly, which seemed to confirm something he had already told her. I was incredibly honored that Wayne Dyer, someone I had long admired for his inspirational words and work, would make himself available to me from the spirit world.

In late 2016, while I was going through the very difficult break up, Anne was there for me. She made time to meet for a few hours at a local café, and I can honestly say her support changed the trajectory of my life. Being able to be open and honest and vulnerable with Anne, and having her reflect back to me what she saw happening in my relationship, was invaluable. She gave me soulful advice and guidance, and validated all the gut feelings I had ever had about the relationship yet chose to ignore. I'm sure my spirit guides were cheering the day I met with Anne.

At some point during our talk we both became aware we were not alone. Both of us keenly felt Wayne Dyer's presence, and I could sense him, leaning with both elbows on the table, devouring our entire conversation and delighting in it.

Suddenly, he presented the image of a butterfly. I thought I understood it, based on what she had told me before about the butterfly being his sign, but this time Wayne was showing me a butterfly tattoo, telling me it was on Anne's ribs. Of course, I would have no way of knowing whether or not she had a tattoo, but he was insistent and so I asked. A tear rolled down her cheek as she nodded, yes. Wayne knew this, and has given me this piece of information as confirmation. The fact her dear friend acknowledged the tattoo was very significant to Anne, because Wayne had only learned of it the very last time she saw him alive. At the time, they discussed how important the symbol of the butterfly was to them both.

Wayne followed up with another image, quick on the heels of the butterfly. It was of him eating carrots out of a little white bowl as he listened to Anne and I talk. I was curious. "Anne, I don't know what this means, but I'm getting this really clear image of Wayne sitting here with us and eating a bowl of carrots."

Anne let out a little gasp and grew teary once more. She explained the last time she and Wayne had shared that same meal together they had been with a large group. Although Wayne and Anne shared a passion for healthy food, Wayne also had a weakness for certain junk foods. That night when some hot, crispy fries arrived at the table to share, Wayne dived right in, but Anne had slapped his hand and said, "Eat your carrots!"

The kind of validations that come from the spirit world continue to amaze and delight. This was a perfect example of receiving a piece of information that, in this case, no one but Anne could possibly know.

That night, when I returned home, I felt better than I had in months and truly believed I had been guided by two masters: one living and one passed. I was honored Wayne Dyer had been engaged in our conversation, and I could sense he was really there to try and help. I felt a genuine caring coming from his spirit.

The next day I had a client scheduled for noon. It was one of my last appointments before Christmas, and the woman I was scheduled to meet had brought me a little present. I had never met her before and thought this such a kind gesture, especially considering so much was currently unraveling in my life. The gift was presented in a small Christmas bag, which contained three chocolates and an orange. I held the orange in my hands, immediately understanding its meaning, but the look on my face must have been misunderstood by my client.

"I'm sorry," she said. "I made cookies yesterday, but all I kept hearing and feeling was that I should bring you an orange. I have no idea why, but it's not a very good Christmas gift, is it?"

"It's the best gift you could have given me," I assured her and went on to ask if she knew who Wayne Dyer was. She had heard of him, but didn't know the story of how he often brought one prop on stage during his live shows: an orange. Wayne used the orange to share an important lesson with his audience: the metaphor that you are an orange. It goes like this: When you are squeezed, pressured, triggered, what is inside is what comes out. If you are fearful or hateful, that is what comes out. If you are full of love, love always comes out. And the important thing is that you have a choice as to what is inside.

Receiving the orange that day, the very morning after my encounter with Wayne in the café with Anne, was to me a clear message. Not only did I know Wayne was with me, guiding and helping me, but I knew he was encouraging me to let go of the anger in my heart and to forgive. To focus on the positive potential of love, and hope and healing, and to leave sadness, hurt, anger, and regret behind. It was such a blessing, and I felt such gratitude this great teacher had shared some of his wisdom with me, through a simple orange.

CHAPTER 23

EMITTUKWET SA'QEWEY NITAP

A VISIT FROM AN OLD FRIEND

Being able to let go of a toxic relationship was freeing. In leaving the relationship I learned to love myself more fully and to trust my gut when it comes to love. I truly feel the experience opened me to a love the likes of which I had never allowed myself to receive. I did find love again, with a beautiful woman named Michelle, and our relationship is by far the healthiest and most balanced relationship of my life. Ours is truly a marriage of equals.

Spending time with Michelle, and falling in love with my best friend, was the greatest gift in the world. I am grateful to the Great Spirit for helping us find each other again.

Fact is, Michelle and I had met seven years prior at a group reading she held at her home in East Chezzetcook, Nova Scotia. I remember thinking she was special at the time, and somebody would be very lucky to have her in their life.

After the relationship with my previous partner ended, I stood outside staring up toward the stars on New Year's Eve. It was December 31, 2016, and as the clock struck midnight I prayed and pleaded with my guides, with the angels, and with the Great Spirit to send the perfect person for me. I was tired of being hurt and wanted somebody I could share my life journey with—and vice versa. Soon after, Michelle and I happened to run into each other at the grocery store, and after a year of being together we got engaged. We purchased a property on the ocean, with plans to build a house, and a life, together.

Until then, I often stayed over at her house. One such night I was in a deep slumber, cuddled right up to Michelle, when I began to dream. Ironically, I was at the grocery store once again. I was standing in the produce section, but could see down near the breads and baked goods. A man was walking toward me, becoming clearer as he got closer. I could see he was wearing a checkered shirt, and his hair was slicked over to the side. All at once, his face became clear.

"Oh my God," I said. "John. John McGrath! How are you? I haven't seen you in such a long time." John and I used to work together in the office of the furniture-manu- facturing plant in Calgary, Alberta. He just smiled and took his time as he walked right past me. John looked great, and younger than I remembered. He walked past a table where three women were sitting. As he did, everything seemed to turn into a restaurant, and I became a waiter. I kept trying to get John to speak to me, but he continued walking past with his happy smile.

I woke up, amazed, and quickly grabbed my phone. After some searching, I discovered John James McGrath had passed away two weeks earlier—January 4, 2018, at the age of 78.

He showed me three women sitting at a restaurant table waiting to be served for a reason. When I read his obituary, there were three women listed, his wife and two daughters. I have a feeling he was asking me to be of service to them if need be. I have reached out to them via online messenger and let them know about the dream. I know without a doubt he loves them very, very much and is watching over them.

I was blown away by the fact he would come to visit and let me know he had made his transition into the light. We all lose contact with people, but never in a million years would I have thought I would find out somebody had moved into the spirit world this way. I am again thankful, and grateful, and know we were in each other's life for a reason. When my day comes, I have a feeling he will be in the vast group of those waiting for me, to greet me and welcome me home.

I say this to many people: "None of us are getting out of this world physically alive." We all have a time to be here, to learn, to grow, and to evolve as a spirit. We are all simply spirits having a sometimes short human experience—not the other way around.

Many can pass through our lives and not seem significant. However, we learn from every person who comes into our lives. We are all connected by the same goal: to help each other grow and accomplish what we need to while we are here. Some people do this in small ways, others in much greater ways. Some people can be our greatest teachers through great hardship, and others through great love.

CHAPTER 24

NEYITA'QL NE'TAPTASIKL
RECEIVING SIGNS

People who are in the spirit world find all kinds of ways to communicate with those of us still here in the physical world. It could be through a butterfly. It could be a dime. It could be a dragonfly. It may even be a perfectly timed and placed feather, a rainbow, or even a dream. Sometimes it's a song on the radio or repeating numbers. For example, you might continually see 11:11 on a clock, or 222 on a license plate. Either way, your loved ones will find a way of communicating via one or more of these intentional signs. If you have many family members or close friends in the spirit world, they will usually send different signs. I know it's my dad who sends dimes because of the image of the ship and his naval background. Also, the dimes I find are usually from 1987—the year he died.

Sometimes, people schedule an appointment to figure out who is behind the signs they are receiving. They come hoping I will validate the sign or symbol as that from a specific spirit.

I always tell them when I receive that image in my readings, but the truth is, you probably already know who the sign is from. Trust your intuition, your psychic vibes, and your heart. Your spirit already knows. In private sessions, I also sometimes ask clients to write down who they think is sending them a particular sign. I also write down who I know it is, based on my communication with the spirit world. Ninety-nine percent of the time we've written down the same name. They already knew, yet they wanted it confirmed. Many people ask, "Why do I find so many dimes?" Dimes are light and easy for a spirit to move, so they are a common sign a spirit is with you. A few weeks after she met with me, one of my clients posted an amazing story on Facebook. During our session her father communicated to me that he sends his daughter dimes. She acknowledged she did find dimes from time to time, but nothing could have prepared her for what happened next. While readying her living room to put up the Christmas tree, she moved an entertainment unit. Behind the unit was a cross, which had belonged to her father. What do you think was perched atop the cross? A dime! The cross had been behind the entertainment unit since the previous Christmas, so how could that possibly have happened without the assistance of a spirit?

Similarly, religious medallions are also light and easy to move. Another client posted a story to Facebook four months after we had met. During our session, four of her recently deceased relatives connected with me and told me they would be sending my client a religious medallion of some kind. Four months later, when she went to visit her brother's grave, there was a medallion of Archangel Michael sitting on his tombstone, waiting for her to find it.

The comfort these two women experienced when they received these signs is beyond measure. I love being able to help people understand that spirits communicate with us all the time, letting us know they are eternally with us.

I also know, without a shadow of a doubt, that spirits listen when you desire a specific form of conformation. Earlier, I wrote about how I asked for a sign from my dad, and knew I could count on him to send dimes and blue jay feathers. I also started to notice he would make sure that wherever I was, in the car, the dentist's office, or the mall, I was sure to hear either "American Pie" or "The House of the Rising Sun," two songs he often sang and played on his guitar.

I was really curious about how far we could take this, so I decided to ask my father for something very specific and very unique. This is when I was still living in Calgary. I knew if he came through with the request it would be an incredible validation that he still heard me. I asked for a bird sighting, but not just any bird. I asked for a pure-white dove. Doves, after all, were not a common sight in Calgary, Alberta. Soon after, I started to notice images of doves appearing on TV commercials, on billboards, and in photos. Once, I even saw one on a truck parked beside me in traffic: Two Doves moving company. I also recall having a conversation with my father in which I said things like, "Dad, I know you're trying, but I don't want a picture of a dove. I want the actual thing. I want to see a real, white dove."

Months passed. One day, I got a call to do a group reading at a house on the other side of Calgary. The city has a major highway, which runs from one end to the other, called Deerfoot Trail, which is what I used to cross Calgary that day. As I drove, I thought about the sign I'd asked my dad for, and how it hadn't yet appeared. I have to admit I was feeling a little disappointed. Just then, "The House of the Rising Sun" came on the radio and I remember thinking, *That's nice, Dad, but I'm still waiting for my dove.* Just as the song finished, I was driving past the Bow River. I looked off to my left and saw a white bird. I was doing 100 kilometers per hour, but the white flash of the bird piqued my curiosity. I kept stealing glances as I drove and, sure enough, it appeared to be heading right for my car.

I was starting to get excited now because the bird was so white. I stole another glance, and as it got closer I realized with a start that it was definitely a dove. Still, it kept coming. That dove ended up flying right beside my driver's side window! As if to seal the deal, it looked me square in the eyes.

I was completely blown away and immediately started to cry. My dad had come through with shining colors! A song called "It's Okay to Cry for Me" aptly played on the radio next. And so I did! I had set the bar high, but he delivered.

The next story is a more recent story, where I hadn't received a dime from my father in a long time.

It was about a month before my 49th birthday and I wanted to have a little conversation with my father, once again, to send me a few dimes. I don't need constant validation that he is still around, but it is nice when it does come. It had been 15 years since the dove appeared in such an undeniable way.

I lit a candle, lit just enough smudge medicine in my smudging shell, smudged myself and offered some of the smudge smoke and medicine to my father in the spirit world. As I offered him the smudge medicine, I spoke clearly to him and said, "Dad, when you get a chance could you send me a couple of dimes in a unique way? Just so I know you are still there."

A few days went by, and eventually a few weeks, and to be honest I had almost forgotten that I asked. It was June 4, 2021—my 49th birthday. The night before my birthday, Michelle told me she had to work. So I planned to have a chill day watching movies on the TV and set a baseball hat on my bedroom dresser the night before. I was just going to relax and enjoy the day.

When I woke up, I went to grab my hat from the dresser where I had placed it the night before. In front of it were two dimes. I thought for a moment that maybe Michelle had placed them there before she went to work. I called her on the phone and asked, "Did you put two dimes in front of my hat before you left for work today?" She said she hadn't, so I told her my story about asking my father for a couple of dimes. I felt strongly that it was him—it was my birthday, after all.

I stood there for a moment looking at the dimes, and thanked my dad for remembering my request and remembering it was my birthday. I could tangibly feel his presence in the room listening to me. As I finished speaking to him, I watched one of the metal handles on the dresser lift up by itself and drop, making a metal clinging sound. To be honest it startled me a bit, then I laughed and teared up for a moment.

I took a picture with my phone to remember that image of the dimes laying in front of my hat on my birthday. I knew when the dresser handle picked up and dropped, that it was his way of saying, "I'm right here with you, son, and I hear you."

I hope these stories help make you more aware that you, too, can speak to your loved ones in the spirit world. Make time to talk to them and include them in your life. If you need a special sign, ask them. Light a candle, light some smudge smoke, and invite them to hear you and your request. Be patient, all good things come in time. Their time in the spirit world is much different than ours; in Spirit there is no time, just the constant present moment. However, they are aware of the times and moments that are special to us, like a birthday or anniversary.

That dove came to me in the most powerful and unique way. I didn't even know if it was possible, but I still asked and believed I would receive. This extraordinary thing happened to me, and I believe I'm no more connected than anyone else—I am just more aware of my connections. Please know you have that same connection to your people, to your loved ones, to your Ancestors in the spirit world. When they deliver their signs, remember to thank them. They like knowing you see the sign for what it actually is: direct communication.

SPEAKING TO YOUR LOVED ONES
IN THE SPIRIT WORLD

I often talk to my dad and loved ones in the spirit world and include them in my life. This exercise is about you, and I want you to be able to have the same connection I do with your loved one in Spirit. To begin, choose a private location where you cannot be disturbed, such as a park bench, under a big tree, a flower garden, or a path in the forest. If you'd like, bring a few pictures or belongings that your loved one once owned and hold them through the process. Allow yourself five minutes (or more) to speak out loud to your loved one. Tell them how you are and what is happening in your life, as if you were catching them up since you last spoke. I would do this with absolute love, kindness, and respect. Be patient and prepared for amazing signs and messages that they will send to let you know they hear you in divine time.

CHAPTER 25

JIJAQMIJK NUJI KLULAJI—TELEVISIONIKTUK NEMITASIK

SPIRIT TALKER— THE TV SERIES

Life unfolds in interesting and meaningful ways, and although I had never sought out to be on television, I did leave it up to the Creator. If I was meant to do a TV show, I would, and if Spirit thought that being in the public eye and showing that spirit connection and communication is real and how possible it is, then I would gladly assist in demonstrating how that process takes place.

Although I was open to the idea of being on television, I didn't actively look for opportunities. I had been approached in the past about a different series, one focused on unsolved murder cases, but it didn't feel like the right project.

Many years later I heard that a History Channel show was being filmed in Nova Scotia called *The Curse of Oak Island,* and I felt a pull to get in touch and offer my input. I called a friend of mine involved in the industry, who was able to give me the contact information of the owner of one of the production companies involved in the show.

I made the call and gave my name. He seemed startled and responded with, "Shawn Leonard? The spirit talker? The medium Shawn Leonard? I just heard about you. I had a conversation about you yesterday! You did a show here locally with another medium named John Holland, and one of my writers was at the show, named Donna Gabriel. She said she had spoken to you several years ago and told me that I should reach out to you, and now here you are reaching out to me. Did she call and tell you to call me?"

I said, "No, I'm calling you because I heard you are co-producing the show on Oak Island, and I'd love to go out there and possibly help out." Ed responded by saying, "Well, I can probably work that out for you, but have you ever thought about doing a TV show, and if you did what that might look like?"

After some back and forth and a couple of conversations with APTN, an Indigenous TV network, Ed reached back out. They were interested in having me do a show for the channel, one that consisted of live shows in Indigenous communities, with additional filmed personal sessions. Ed explained, "We're thinking about calling it *Spirit Talker* since your Indigenous name is White Eagle Spirit

Talker, and professionally you call yourself a spirit talker. They love that title, and the premise."

We filmed the pilot episode in Listuguj, and it was a great show. I read several people in the audience, and it was while we were there filming the pilot that I met Tracey Metallic. She was there with another woman, and while I was doing the live show, I connected to Tracey's uncle who was in spirit. I mentioned to her that he was a photographer, which led me to vibe out Tracey, and I quickly realized that she was also an artist.

After I connected to her during the live event, she showed me some of her work, which I absolutely loved. I told her that one day I hoped that we could collaborate on a project together and expressed my desire to one day create an oracle card deck. Several years later, we are doing just that.

These kinds of synchronistic moments have been a recurring theme in my life, and I have found that when you are in alignment with your true purpose, the Creator will collaborate with you to create a life that you never even dreamed possible.

Spirit Talker is now in its fourth season, which I feel may be the last. In Indigenous culture, four is a sacred number. There are four directions on the medicine wheel, the hoop of life, and I feel that four seasons would best represent who I am, and what it is that I do. If four seasons is the end, I would be happy I had the opportunity to share my work with the world in this way.

Although I never sought having my own television series, I did put out the intention that I wanted to share my wisdom and knowledge. My hope was that others might be able to shift their perspective in such a way that they could experience life with the full understanding that we are Spirit having a human experience. I didn't have to compromise the message I wanted to convey to the world, and I allowed the opportunity to unfold in my life rather than force it to happen.

When you are in alignment with Spirit you notice those synchronistic moments happen more often, and you begin to see how meaningful "chance" encounters can truly be. When you realize how safe and protected you are and release your fears, opportunities will present themselves without having to seek them out; they will simply come to you.

Embarking on the *Spirit Talker* TV series journey was a gift. I had the chance to go to different Indigenous communities and meet many people, including knowledge keepers and Elders. I was not raised in an Indigenous community, and felt my prayer for cultural knowledge was being answered.

I would learn about the beautiful and unique perspectives and customs that exist within the varied Indigenous communities found within Canada. I offered healing as a gift to the communities that I visited and they would in turn connect me to Elders who would teach me about a community's culture. It was incredibly rewarding, and the start of a new spiritual journey for me.

CHAPTER 26

NEPITASIKL
SA'QEWE'L LA'QNN

HEALING
GENERATIONAL WOUNDS

When people connect with a spirit talker, it's because they are seeking to connect with their loved ones in Spirit, and there is immense healing that can take place because of that communication.

I receive information through the "Clairs": clairsentience, clairaudience, claircognizance, clairalience, and clairgustance—the psychic language by which Spirit communicates.

I will speak about this universal communication in more detail in later chapters.

The messages and information that come through can affect me mentally and emotionally. Oftentimes, those who come to see me are deeply impacted by trauma, which can span across many generations in the form of family karma. These issues have a way of rippling outward, affecting the lives of the generations that follow as well, which creates systemic issues that can be extremely overwhelming.

In the final episode of my second season of *Spirit Talker*, I encountered my most difficult reading to date on the television series regarding the emotional nature of the messages that came through that day. While I was in Blomidon, Nova Scotia—Glooscap First Nation, I was able to meet with Darlene and her daughter Kyra, and during the reading Darlene's mother, Vivian, came through and expressed that she had passed away when Darlene was still very young.

She communicated that Darlene had been taken from her life and was unable to be with her mother at the time of her passing. Vivian had also expressed how sorry she was about being unable to be there for her daughter in the way that she had wanted to be. Darlene had been placed in a child institution and she was unable to be with her mother because of this.

Darlene was 12 years old when her mother died of alcoholism, which stemmed from sexual abuse Vivian had experienced from a priest when she was just a child herself. As a result of generational trauma, Darlene began to struggle with addiction as well, after the sudden passing of her father.

Vivian provided insight through the messages she conveyed, which helped me better understand her journey, and how lost she had felt during her life. Having said that though, when I looked into Darlene's eyes, I could see wisdom and light. She had been through so much and had walked a journey through darkness and found light within herself once again.

Her Ancestors were present during the reading and wanted me to communicate with her that they had been through it all with her. They had watched over her and had walked with her in life. They loved her so incredibly and were with her throughout her journey—even when she struggled in the darkness.

Although there were moments in her life when she could have died, Spirit prevented that from happening. Somehow her Ancestors and loved ones, including her mother, helped Darlene divert and change things. She had heard a voice inside her telling her to make certain choices to keep her safe. Vivian also expressed enormous pride for her daughter, and how Darlene was able to overcome so much in life, and that her biggest wish was for Darlene to find her way through it all.

Prior to the reading, I had specified to Spirit that I wanted only Kyra's and Darlene's relatives to communicate with me, but as I spoke to the mother and daughter a loud rattling sound could be heard off camera near the curtain behind me. The voice of a woman yelling could also be heard on set, but unfortunately it wasn't picked up on the mics even though all the crew could hear a disembodied voice of a woman. Someone in Spirit had begun to shake a light fixture above our heads to get our attention. In that moment, Vivian showed me the image of a toaster, and when I told Kyra what I saw in my mind's eye she instantly broke down into tears.

It was an image that evoked shame within her. She hadn't been comfortable talking about it, and it was a device she had used for self-harm. Kyra is an Indigenous sovereignty activist who is learning to walk her path in life in a good and positive way and recently has graduated from university. Her grandmother was immensely proud of her but brought this image up for a reason. Although they had never met in life, Vivian wanted Kyra to not only know that her grandmother was fully aware of the challenges her granddaughter had faced in life but that she also wanted her to heal these ancestral wounds.

Up until this point in the reading, Vivian had been communicating with me directly, but Kyra's close friend Angela wanted to express a message. It was her voice that we heard on set, and she shook the light fixture in a desperate attempt to communicate with me. She showed me the image of a tree-lined field, which strongly resonated with Kyra because she had been assaulted in a field on a family friend's property. Kyra's friend Angela had passed away on October 19, 2017, at the age of 17, after she took her own life due to trauma she had experienced herself.

Kyra is two-spirit, an Indigenous term for someone with both a masculine and feminine spirit, and was in love with her friend Angela but had never told her while she was alive. Angela had been dating someone else, so Kyra never expressed her true feelings. Both had been through similar situations of abuse, and Angela could see and feel that Kyra was struggling now in her life.

Spirit wanted me to help this young woman and what better way to assist in the healing process than to show me what and where caused her so much pain and hurt in life. Angela guided and showed me where Kyra needed healing the most. This way Kyra could work with her emotions that she had kept bottled up inside herself, and finally heal what had caused so much pain. There is nothing that goes unseen in Spirit, and they know where and how we hurt.

As a spirit talker, I help bridge these worlds and assist in helping people connect to their loved ones, and I want you to be able to do that in your own life. I feel we are all being called to be in service in one way or another, to be a source of light in dark times, and to help heal those who need healing when we feel called to do so. There is so much to be gained from knowing that we don't die, and that there is so much more to life than this physical reality. Our bodies may no longer be living in this world, but our essence—our spirit—continues. Our loved ones in Spirit love us unconditionally and want us to heal, and that's why they bring forth the messages that need to be healed the most.

Meeting with a medium or spirit talker can help somebody face issues they have been ignoring, or have been silently struggling with; something that they have been emotionally bearing, harboring guilt about, or issues that have caused them to be angry. It's about being available to help people move the energy within themselves so that they can facilitate their own healing. This is just one step, though, and those individuals need to continue stepping forward every day until they are living presently and loving themselves unconditionally.

Angela was making it apparent that Kyra would end that cycle. That she would end that pattern of inherited trauma, and that the strides she had taken in her life would break that cycle for her family's descendants so that they would be protected, and in doing so she would help heal the Ancestors that came before her.

Systemic issues for Indigenous people are vast and complex and impact people in a multitude of ways— abuse, addictions, poverty, and more. The karma associated with these issues has a way of being passed down to future generations until that cycle stops. Vivian, Darlene, Angela, and Kyra had all experienced abuse during their childhoods, and this karma had been passed down from generation to generation. Kyra was ultimately healing her family line: past, present, and future, so that any children born within their family going forward would be free of those traumatic experiences.

Unfortunately, throughout Canadian history Indigenous peoples who attempted to practice traditions, cultural customs, and speak their own language were met with unjust cruelty. There are many examples of this, but one is that of province-sanctioned residential schools that operated for more than 160 years, until 1996. They were part of a broader plan and a means for the aggressive assimilation, colonization, and genocide of the Indigenous people of Canada. More than 150,000 children passed through the doors of these institutions, and they were abused either verbally, physically, or sexually, and many died from disease, neglect, or suicide. The tragedy of this genocide is far-reaching and ripples outward through each generation.

My belief is that healing is possible only when those cycles of trauma end, and it is through education, reconnection to cultural roots, and releasing the pain associated with those wounds that healing can truly take place for the Indigenous people of Turtle Island. As a spirit talker, I am so fortunate to meet with many Indigenous people who are doing just that, who are making a difference in their own lives and the lives of future generations. It serves as a great reminder that, ultimately, love is the answer, and true healing is available for everyone.

I pray that everyone who reads this book can heal and find strength in whatever situations they find themselves in. That if they are struggling in life, they find the courage to heal and move past the belief that they can't change their life circumstances, so that they can heal their own family lines and move through life in a more unconditional loving, healthy, and positive way.

A PRAYER FOR INTERGENERATIONAL HEALING

Great Spirit, Creator, and all Ancestors, hear my words and heart.

I ask you to enlighten and help all people heal who are affected by generational trauma.

I ask you to assist all people move through their mental, emotional, and sometimes physical pain to a space of acceptance, peace, and unconditional love for self and all others.

Enlighten all of us to rise above the hurts of the past, present, and potential future.

Help all of us end the cycle and break the continued karma and life experiences affected by generational trauma.

I ask for your light to shine in the darkness and let there be no shadow unhealed.

Help us to remember the past and teach others from it so this may never happen again to any person of any race, creed, or culture.

Help us be proud and speak our languages and celebrate our Indigenous culture.

Help us remember we are all Indigenous to this planet, and we are all one.

Thank you, all my relations, for hearing my words and prayer.

Wela'lin, Msit No'kmaq

CHAPTER 27

No'kmaq na Tekweywijik

My Ancestors Are With Me

We all need breaks or vacations in life to help us stay balanced and grounded, and the islands of Hawaii have helped replenish my mind, body, and spirit during my stays there. During our last stay on the Big Island of Hawaii my fiancé, Michelle, her daughter Ashley, and myself stayed at a place along the coastline. We were on the west side of the island where it doesn't rain as much and stayed on the third floor of a building overlooking the beautiful sights of the North Pacific Ocean; it was an incredible location, and a nice place to feel spiritually connected.

There is something almost otherworldly about Hawaii, and one prominent feature are the active volcanoes located on the islands. One evening we decided to go for a drive and watch the sunset. When we arrived, I stood outside, and I thought to myself how fortunate I was to be standing in one of the most beautiful places on Earth. My thoughts then drifted to Wayne Dyer, and how he often spoke of Maui. He would often write about how it felt like heaven on Earth—that it was the closest he could be to heaven while still living here on Earth, and I understand how he felt because I feel the same way.

In that moment I thought about my Ancestors, and about how we all have many people that we love who were part of our lives that are no longer here physically. These Ancestors transcend even this lifetime, and our connections to them expand into our many other lifetimes as well. Even with the countless number of lives we live, all our Ancestors remain with us.

As I stood in one of the most beautiful locations in the world, I called upon them while I was standing on top of this mountain; I spoke to the spirit world out loud, as I often do, and I asked for my father and my grandmother, and my great-grandparents. I spoke to my aunt Nancy, and I asked her to be there as well. I invited all my loved ones and Ancestors in Spirit to spend time with me during my stay in Hawaii.

I felt that because Hawaii is such a peaceful and spiritual place, because it always helps me refocus and assists in rejuvenation, that it would be amazing if they could all be there with me. I had never thought to invite my Ancestors from this lifetime and the many other lifetimes I have lived before, so I invited them all to be there with me. I spoke my request out loud, and then I let it go. I could sense them there, and I could feel their presence because there is an energy when you speak to Spirit out loud and from your heart. You can feel their awareness standing right there with you.

In the morning, we sat out on our balcony enjoying the beautiful scenery, smelling the fresh sea air, and hearing the ocean and the sounds of doves cooing. There was something powerful about the moment, which made me think about my invitation to my Ancestors from the night before.

I thought of my request that they be included on this trip, and in that moment I looked up and noticed a white feather floating down from the sky. It was maybe half an inch long, and it continued to float down past our balcony almost in slow motion.

It passed us and as I watched it float down to the floor below us, suddenly, through clairaudience, I heard a voice say, "Shawn, hold out your hand." So I took out my left hand, and I held it out in front of me with my palm facing upward. At that moment the feather floated vertically back up to us; we were watching as it moved directly toward me and landed right in the center of my palm.

I'm never really surprised when things like this happen. They don't happen every day, but when they do it's incredible. I thought back to the invitation I had said out loud to my loved ones and Ancestors the night before, and how I spoke from my heart while standing on top of that volcano, and this feather was the validation that I needed in that moment to remind me that they heard every word I had spoken. It wasn't a subtle message from Spirit, but a resounding message saying, "We are with you!"

The experience I had with the feather reaffirmed to me that our Ancestors are always with us, and it isn't just from this lifetime, but from our vast number of lifetimes as well. We just need to speak to them and remember that they are there. It's okay to invite them on our journey, and to include them in the amazing things that we do. They want to be included and remembered because they are always there guiding and loving us.

When you learn to trust that your Ancestors walk alongside you in this life, you notice a deeper relationship and communication with them. Ask for validation so that they can hear your requests, and you will be amazed by their ability to communicate messages to you. They will hear you, and they will validate that you have been heard, whether it be through a sign in the form of a feather or a voice in your mind that asks you to hold out your hand. I know that if it can happen for me, then it can happen for you.

A PRAYER FOR ANCESTORIAL CONNECTION

My immediate family and Ancestors who are in the spirit world, hear my heartfelt words and prayer.

I invite you to be with me this day as today is a special day, and I wish to share this moment with you.

I have not forgotten you, and today in this moment I celebrate our relation and continued connection.

I request you take a moment of time from your place where there is no time to spend with me.

I am grateful and appreciate your unconditional love and presence.

I thank you all, with great love and respect, all my relations.

Weliaoq Msit No'kmaq

CHAPTER 28

JIJAQMIJE'K
MELKIKNA'TITE'WK
WAIS+SK

SPIRIT POWER ANIMAL

As I have grown spiritually and more connected to my cultural roots it has become apparent to me that we share this world with many nations, and they work in balance to create harmony for all of Mother Earth's inhabitants. These include the human, plant, spirit, mineral, and animal nations. The human nation embodies the diverse cultures of people that share our planet and help us recognize the beauty in our differences. The plant nation encompasses all the trees and natural medicines that grow in our world that provide us with the opportunity for healing, along with the food we eat. The spirit nation connects us to our Ancestors, guides, and loved ones in Spirit, and to the Creator. The mineral nation makes up the mountains and the soil we stand upon on Mother Earth and contains its sacred grounding energy.

The animal nation is the focus for my next story, showing how our connection to animals transcends to a spiritual level as well. The animals that reside on Mother Earth walk alongside us; we share the same resources and live in the same physical world as them. Some animals sustain us through the food they provide, and other times as companions with the unconditional love they offer. Whether or not we know this to be true, we all have a sacred connection to the animal world.

All living things have a light within them. Animals can be messengers. Sometimes people may look at a bumblebee or a cardinal or a lizard and feel that it connects to them personally or know that it is a loved one in Spirit who has brought forth a message. Even among the animal world there are specific nations that can often reveal their connection to us in unique and profound ways. I was given this knowledge that helped me understand our collective connection to animals in a spiritual sense, and on a personal level what animals support me along my spiritual journey in this life.

One night, a dream came to me. I was not experiencing much stress in my life at that time and had been sleeping soundly. I woke up within my dream, very much aware of my surroundings, and realized that I was standing in the middle of a field.

I noticed seven shadowy figures running toward me, and I felt that I was in danger. I didn't know who or what these shadows were, but I decided that if I could outrun them and make it to the tree line ahead of me that I would likely be safe. I felt like I was running for my life in this dream, and I ran as fast as I could, but I could not outrun them, and they continued to keep the same pace as me.

I knew I would have to surrender, but before I was forced to, I looked across the field to the area that I was running toward. I saw seven polar bears appear, all of which started to run toward me, and immediately the seven shadowy figures that had been chasing me began to run in the opposite direction. At that point I thought, *"Oh my God. I probably have a better chance running from these guys than I do running toward polar bears,"* since the bears were so massive, and the dream felt so incredibly real.

The shadows that had been chasing me had now begun to run as well, but they were now sprinting away from the polar bears. I was trying to outrun these dark figures, but they were already ahead of me, and as I made it to the center of the field, I realized that I could not outrun the bears—they were moving way too fast.

I stopped and stood still, having accepted the fact that these great, white bears would overtake me. As I stopped, the shadowy figures kept running away, and to my surprise the polar bears swiped or pounced at these shadow figures, and as they did the shadows disintegrated before my eyes. They were no longer there, and as the last bear jumped onto the last shadow all seven animals stepped into each other and merged into one great and powerful polar bear. This animal stared back at me, and I realized in that moment that this bear was not there to hurt me but was here to help, and that's when I woke up.

I knew immediately that my dream was important, an epiphany moment in my life. I realized that the polar bear was my *power* totem spirit animal, and just like how the eagle is my *spirit* totem animal and has also played a significant role in my journey through life, the spirit of the polar bear was letting me know that I was protected.

Many eagle feathers—and even a wing—have made their way to me. I feel deeply connected to the eagle, which is also part of my Indigenous name, White Eagle Spirit Talker, or Wape'k Kitpu Aknutmajik Jijaqmij in Mi'kmaq. That name was given to me during a naming ceremony, and it is how I identify myself in Indigenous circles and ceremonies.

My belief is that we all have a spirit totem animal and power animal; in the same way the eagle connects to my spiritual life and is thus my spirit totem animal, our power totem animals help protect us from the struggles we go through. My dream was significant, and I immediately felt this deep connection to the polar bear that I had never felt before. I know they're one of the most powerful land animals in the world, and after this dream I began searching for a deeper connection to the polar bear.

I thought to myself that I would love to have a polar bear claw to remind me of that special connection we share. So I asked the Creator and spoke to the great, white bear spirit, hoping that somehow they could send me a claw. I wanted to have validation that the polar bear was my power animal. I put it out to the Creator and the spirit world and then I let it go. I told my partner, Michelle, that I didn't know how this was going to happen, but that I was hopeful and optimistic. After a few months had gone by, a friend and student of mine named Barbara was visiting Labrador, Newfoundland, where she met an Elder who had given her two polar bear claws.

He told her that he was giving her two claws because one was meant for her and the other was to be gifted to someone else. He explained the story behind the bear's passing, that it had been killed humanely by Innu hunters, and that there was no malicious intent surrounding its death. When he told Barbara that the other claw was to be gifted, my name immediately came to mind.

She carefully wrapped the claw in a red piece of fabric—a very Indigenous way to wrap a gift, as red represents divine protection for sacred items—and included a very nice card. When I opened the little parcel from her, I was immediately surprised and overwhelmed to see what was inside. There was my polar bear claw; it had found its way to me. I know my prayers and words are always heard, and it has enormous meaning for me. She even had the claw wrapped in rope with a few wooden beads so I could wear it close to my heart; I know I will wear it for the rest of my life.

About a month after I received this treasured gift, I had some friends over to my home, including one who does some part-time taxidermy work. Lori had heard me speak about receiving the claw, and she had recently discovered an extra piece of polar bear fur at her shop in Enfield, Nova Scotia, but it was too small for her to use so she gifted it to me, saying that she felt it was important that I wrap the claw in the piece of fur whenever I was not wearing it. She gave it to me wrapped in a red cloth, just as the claw came to me, and my eagle wing before that.

Shortly after I received the polar bear fur, my friend Jasmin reached out to me and mentioned that a woman she knew nearby had a polar bear rug that she wanted to give away. So I reached out and asked if I could come by to look at it, telling her I was Indigenous, and when I arrived at her home she immediately realized who I was.

I am well known in this neck of the woods, and she was surprised it was me. She mentioned that she had wanted a reading with me for years, but since I stopped doing personal readings, she was unable to. She asked if she could give me the polar bear rug in exchange for a reading for her and her mom, and I happily agreed.

Since I spoke my desire to receive a claw to the Creator, my guides, my angels, and to the spirit of the polar bear itself, I have been gifted parts from three different bears. These parts have appeared to me, and I often marvel about how special it was to receive these gifts, and about how their energy has abundantly flowed into my life. The dream I experienced and the connection I have to my power animal has confirmed to me its significance to my life. When they merged into one bear I feel it was to symbolize that we are all one. As true as that statement is within the human nation, it is also the case among the bear nation.

I don't see things as accidents, and I do believe that those seven bears that appeared in my dream were in the spirit world at the time that I encountered them. I also feel I will receive seven parts from those seven bears at some point in my life; throughout my journey, those seven bears will come into my life in one physical form or another. I feel they knew who I was long before I was made aware of their presence.

My spirit totem animal is the eagle and I feel deeply connected to eagles spiritually; the polar bear is my power totem animal, and I constantly feel protected by them in my life. However, it is my belief that the spiritual connection I have to the animal world is in every one of us. It is not just for Indigenous people. Indigenous people may experience it more strongly, but everyone has a spiritual connection to the animal nation, no matter your cultural background.

Before we live our lives and before we choose our path in this life, these animals are already deeply connected to us—even without our awareness of them. These are spiritual animals with a connection to all of us, and once you are made aware of their presence and this knowledge is presented to you, take special care to include their power in all that you do.

When you pray to your guides and angels, remember to include your spirit totem animals and power totem animals. The power they can provide to you, that they exemplified in their own life, can help support you in your journey as well.

Once you remember and reconnect to your own spirit totem animal and power totem animal it will enrich your life as much as it has enriched my own. I walk through life each day knowing that not only do I have the wisdom and help of my spirit guides, angels, and Ancestors, but that I also walk with the connection of my spirit totem animal Wabek Kitpu, white eagle, and my power totem animal Wabek Muin, polar bear.

We all share a connection to the animal world, but how can you know which animals are your spirit totem and power animals? You might have felt a pull to a particular animal without knowing the reason behind it. Or perhaps you've had unusual experiences with a certain animal that seems unexplainable, which may be a sign of their connection to you. Nevertheless, they are here to help you through your journey in this life, and if you speak to them from the heart, and request to know which animals are connected to you, they will give you signs to let you know who they are.

By knowing about your own personal connection to these animals, it allows you to deepen your existing connection to them so that you have additional spiritual support to call upon in life and during moments of prayer and reflection. As they offer their strength to you along your journey, trust in the wisdom that they will impart, and the protection they so freely provide. We are never alone in this life, and the support we receive from the other side is unfathomable. So, speak to your angels, guides, Ancestors, Spirit, and totem animals, and remember they are always walking this path with you, and are protecting you in your journey in this life.

SPIRIT TOTEM ANIMAL MEDITATION

Please sit or lie in a comfortable space and location, where you will not be disturbed.

Ask the Creator and Ancestors to surround you with an unconditional loving light of divine guidance and protection.

Close your eyes and take three slow, deep breaths. That's right, just relax.

Now envision yourself with your psychic inner eyes, standing on a path in a large open field.

At the end of the path, you can see the path continues down into the forest.

I want you to walk down the path as you slowly count down from ten to one.

When you reach one, you will be standing at the edge of the forest and completely relaxed.

In your mind, I want you to ask that your spirit totem animal or spirit power totem animal reveal itself to you.

Take your first impression; it may be just a glimpse at first.

Just allow this beautiful animal to come to you and completely embrace you with unconditional love.

You and this great spirit animal have known each other prior to this lifetime, perhaps many lifetimes.

Thank them and welcome their spiritual medicine on your continued journey.

Now count yourself up from one to three and come back to full consciousness.

You will be able to call upon their help and spiritual medicine anytime you require.

CHAPTER 29

MUSQANAMUKSIT JI'NM
THE BLUE MAN

My stepdad, Larry, taught me some great lessons that I have carried with me since he made his journey home, and I have become more aware that the Creator and the universe have a divine plan that we don't always know or fully understand. Since his passing, I've had time to reflect on what I've learned and have made some realizations about how the spirit world perceives energy—especially when connecting to a spirit talker like myself.

This is not only the case for those who have crossed over; it is also true for earthbound spirits who feel reluctant to transition to the other side. The reality is that our energy often precedes our physical bodies, so it's important to connect to our own energetic selves to help better understand those who have passed on, those we interact with in our day-to-day worlds, and, most importantly, ourselves—for all of us to become more spiritually enlightened individuals.

After the discovery of Larry's cancer, the doctors ordered emergency surgery on his brain to remove a mass, which unfortunately led to the realization that the cancer had not originated there but had spread throughout his body prior to that initial discovery. Learning that the energetic dark spot I had witnessed in his aura was indeed cancer was confirmation of what I had seen. I think I was in denial when I saw it. I had prayed that I was wrong and that it wasn't cancer but, unfortunately, it was.

After the surgery was completed and while Larry was still sedated our family went to the hospital to visit him. There were a few doctors and nurses present and as I walked past the curtains that partitioned the area off, Larry noticed me. I could tell he was heavily medicated and wasn't able to communicate the way he typically would, but as soon as he saw me his face lit up and he smiled.

He pointed toward me and excitedly said, "The blue man!" He was trying to explain to everyone in the room who I was, gesturing to the doctors that "the blue man" was there. I wasn't wearing blue clothing at the time, but his response to my presence was different from how he reacted to the rest of our family.

I wasn't surprised that Larry saw me differently than everyone else in the room since my reality can be a bit strange, and I've come to realize that I move through life in a way that is unlike most people. Sometimes the universe teaches me lessons through unique and unusual ways, which makes sense because I experience the world so differently. I think Larry was able to perceive energy in a special way that day and could see my aura when normally he couldn't. Spirit talkers often have auras that contain more blue hues than others. Light blue is connected to the throat chakra and deals with communication, and it connects to the ability to hear spiritually. So, even on an energetic level it may be a way for those who are in the light to distinguish who can relay messages to their loved ones, and who cannot.

It's not unheard of for people who have experienced brain injuries to suddenly tap into skills that were not always present before, and the medical condition acquired savant syndrome came to mind after my experience with Larry. There have been many documented cases of people suddenly being able to play music on a virtuoso level after a traumatic brain injury or suddenly expertly skilled in areas without prior knowledge. The reality is, there is a lot about the human brain we just don't know, and the surgery obviously impacted Larry's ability to perceive energy that day.

The reality is our energy and aura field provide a lot of information that we cannot see, and often don't consciously perceive. I believe some people are more sensitive to this energy, and the same is true for babies or animals. I find as we grow up, we typically become more attached to physical reality and begin to forget our own divinity and our own connection to the spirit world, but small children and animals can instantly sense who they like and who they don't like—because they don't have egos that can impact their perceptions. You might experience this in your own life and find small children or animals feel at home in your presence, and it's likely because they see or sense your aura and feel comfortable around you.

As a species, humans have developed and become more reliant on outside sources for survival and have become less aware of the energy of their environments.

From a societal standpoint, it isn't necessary to focus on these senses nowadays, so often people don't notice subtle changes or feel in tune with the natural world.

We've all met individuals in our lives who we have instantly felt a connection to, or just didn't seem to click with, and I feel it all relates to our energy field and our auras. It's why we often choose the company of certain people over others—it all relates back to energy.

Through my work as a spirit talker, I've noticed that the impressions I pick up from other people are often based on their auras, which provide details about the people I'm speaking to. These are impressions that can't be obtained through the physical senses, but sometimes I can tell what's going on in their lives: like if a person is newly married, if they love people or prefer the company of animals, if they feel depressed or feel stuck in life, and even if they are suffering from an illness. In my experience each person's aura is unique. In the same way everyone's personality is very individual to them, this is also true for what we emit out into the world.

Auras are the sacred light energy that surrounds all living matter and encompasses our physical bodies; they are a subtle emanation of who we are. Our auras are an egg-shaped energetic field, a "force" that exists around the body that is strongly associated with the chakra system. It emits energy in all directions and manifests itself as a field that surrounds our bodies. Some people are more sensitive to the energy of others, but through practice you can become more aware of your own energy and strengthen your ability to see, feel, and perceive auras.

SEEING YOUR AURA

You can use this exercise to help increase your ability to see your own aura. I suggest sitting in a dimly lit room, since direct sunlight can make it more difficult for you to see the energy. It's best if you have a blank wall—preferably one that is a neutral color, such as gray or white.

Begin by closing your eyes. Once you are relaxed focus on your inner vision and imagine the space between your brows, or third eye, expanding energetically. Now reopen your eyes and look at the neutral space you have created. Take a deep breath in and then exhale, and then close your eyes again. Now, reopen your eyes and place your hands in front of you so that the neutral area you have created is in the background behind your hands. With your two pointer fingers facing tip to tip, and about one inch apart, stare at the space between. With your eyes slightly unfocused maintain looking at the space between your fingers. Move your fingers closer together, than farther apart, and you will begin to see a line of energy that connects the two together.

The more you practice this exercise, the more you will feel comfortable maintaining focus and concentration. You can even try the same technique in total darkness and might still be able to see the energy since it's about perceiving clairvoyantly rather than using your physical eyes.

I've come to learn about many healing modalities over the course of my life, and I will touch on another energetic principle that is closely connected to our auras: the chakra system.

We are energetic beings living in an energetic universe; everything material and nonmaterial is made up of energy and possesses its own personal energy field. That includes our auras, the auras of animals, and even rocks and trees—we are all within that larger universal field of energy that surrounds and permeates all existence. Chakras play an important role within our energetic bodies. The term itself is first seen in the Hindu religious texts, the Vedas, and as such the word itself is derived from the Sanskrit word for wheel and represents energy points in the body. They are thought to be spinning disks of energy that should remain open, aligned, and balanced, as they correspond to certain aspects of our physical bodies, which are linked to our emotional and energetic well-being. Each chakra corresponds to a different color, name, number, function, and a specific area of the spine.

In Indigenous culture we understand we are star people and beings . . . meaning light beings made from the stars. We are all physically created from stardust and light that has existed within our galaxy and the universe itself.

The starlight within your chakra system emanates out into your aura. White light through a prism displays a spectrum of seven main colors. You would not have an aura without a connection to the chakras system itself and vice versa. They are both interconnected and are seen and experienced in different ways, just as light through a prism.

It was my experience with Larry and seeing his cancer and illness within his aura and chakra that helped me understand this connection. The black smoke and shadow I saw on the back of Larry's head is what brought my attention to the connection between our aura and the chakra system. Understanding your chakras and aura and the spectrum of light that exists within all of us is pretty amazing. Working with this energy we may be able to heal ourselves and others.

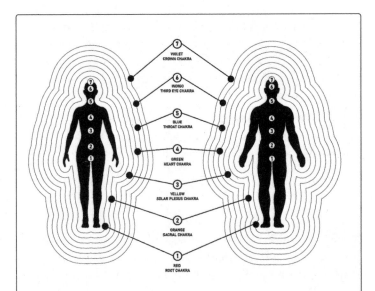

The Root Chakra is found at the base of the spine and is red in color and is the area responsible for feeling grounded and balanced.

The Sacral Chakra is located two finger widths below your naval and is orange in color, and relates to desire, creativity, and sexual energy.

The Solar Plexus Chakra is located three finger widths above the navel and is yellow in color and connects to self-confidence, vitality, and self-control. It connects to clairsentience or "clear feeling."

The **Heart Chakra** is found over the heart and is green in color. It connects to unconditional love, joy, and compassion. It helps link the mind, body, and spirit together.

The **Throat Chakra** is found over the throat and is a light sky-blue color. It is associated with communication, creativity, and sound, and connects to clairaudience or "clear hearing."

The **Third Eye Chakra** is found between the brows and is indigo in color. It is connected to intuition and a higher level of consciousness and works closely with the throat and crown chakras. It is connected to clairvoyance or "clear seeing."

The **Crown Chakra** is found on top of the head and is either violet or white. It is connected to unity, universal wisdom, and open-mindedness. It allows us to connect to higher states of consciousness.

Each chakra system is independent from one another, but their functions blend into each other so that the mind, body, and spirit can be balanced. When the centers are in sync, they work together and act as a unified whole. This ensures that any blockages, excesses, or deficiencies are worked through before they can adversely impact the physical body. It's important to realize that if one aspect of your aura needs to be worked on, the rest of the system should be balanced and aligned as well. This way the energy flows positively throughout, and you're not just focusing on one aspect of the whole.

I recommend doing some research and investigating your own aura and chakras, and learning how to balance your own energy for yourself. As you develop and practice by occasionally raising and lowering your vibration, it can only help you become a more spiritually healthy person. From my work as a spirit talker, I have learned how important our auras are, and how necessary it is to raise and lower your chakras, not only for psychic development but also to help maintain a more balanced approach to life and, by proxy, a balanced approach to your well-being.

As you grow your connection and become more sensitive to the energy that surrounds us all, it's important to maintain healthy spiritual practices. By learning more about your own aura and chakras, and by periodically raising and lowering your energy, you will find how much these exercises will assist you in your pursuit of fulfillment and spiritual enlightenment.

I am forever grateful to Larry and the lessons he taught me. I have found that his journey home helped me learn so much about the divine will of the universe, but also how it allowed me to experience energy in new and important ways. Without his ability to see my aura that day I might have not been so open to receive that message from Spirit—about how our auras are perceived on an energetic level—and would not be able to share this experience with all of you. My hope is that these stories might spark the light within you, and that you choose to delve more into your own energetic bodies, so that you, too, can find ways to better enrich your own lives.

CHAPTER 30

Msit No'kmaq

ALL MY RELATIONS

We are all one, and each person comes from the same source. It is my belief that all spiritual faiths and systems are just different ways of expressing that same energy. They are simply different energetic roads that lead to the same destination, and it's through divine love, which unites us all, that all spiritual beliefs come together. Within Indigenous culture, all ceremonies are done to honor the Great Spirit and our Ancestors. It is through our language, prayers, and customs, and how we speak our words that we connect to the Creator.

Msit No'kmaq means "all my relations" in Mi'kmaq and represents our connection to all things, and all nations. So, when I say all my relations, I'm referring to the interconnectedness of everything, and the complex and balanced interaction that exists among the Creator, Grandfather Sun, Mother Earth, the Mineral Nation, the

Plant Nation, the Animal Nation, the Human Nation, and the Spirit Nation.

It is this symbiotic relationship that connects all nations and allows us to experience oneness and harmony within it all. It reminds us to look at life in a good way, and with unconditional love. In that way we can learn to focus on our connection to it all and acknowledge how these nations come together to help us. This means we respect Mother Earth and her inhabitants, and all aspects of life. We show respect to the spirit world through our prayers and intentions, and by respecting ourselves through our thoughts and actions.

We are one nation evolving from one another and yet still dependent on the Great Spirit, the universe above, and Mother Earth below. "All my relations" is a prayer of oneness and harmony with all forms of life. It is the connection between everything, and it helps us to have the experience of life by supporting each other in a more understanding way.

The Medicine Wheel

The medicine wheel represents all of creation, and the interconnectedness of all people and things within our world. I've been taught by many Elders that each of the Nations who use the medicine wheel within their own specific culture has a unique perspective on how those teachings look. I utilize Mi'kmaq traditions since that is part of who I am, and I honor my Ancestors who came before me.

The wheel's shape represents creation and the circle of life, since there is no beginning and no end. This symbolizes that we are all united, and that we are all one. All

Mi'kmaq ceremonies begin in the east where the sun rises and are performed in a clockwise direction to follow the same path as the sun, moving from the east into the south, through the west and ending in the north.

Each quadrant of the medicine wheel connects to the cardinal directions: east, south, west, and north; the four colors: yellow, red, black, and white; the phases of life: infancy, youth, adulthood, and Elder; the seasons: spring, summer, fall, and winter; the four sacred medicines: Tobacco, Cedar, Sage, and Sweetgrass; the four elements: fire, water, earth, air; the human nation: Asian, Indigenous, African, and Caucasian; and our four-dimensional bodies: spiritual, emotional, physical, wisdom, and truth.

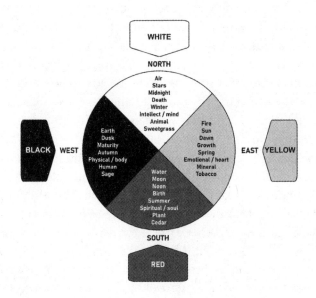

The Seven Directions

The Seven Directions involve those same principles as the medicine wheel's four cardinal directions, but they include the additional directions: above embodied by the Grandfather Sun, below connecting us to Mother Earth, and within allowing us to focus inwardly on ourselves.

The number seven is important to Indigenous culture and to the Mi'kmaq people. We have the Seven Directions, the Seven Sacred Grandfather teachings, and we honor the Seven Generations that have come before us and the seven that will follow. The Seven Directions are used in our ceremonies and are an extension of the teachings within the medicine wheel.

An example of this is when we take part in a water ceremony and we sing our water songs, we are singing to the water that moves through the east. We sing to the water that flows through the south, to the water residing in the west, and the water that exists in the north direction. We simultaneously sing to the water above, the water below, and the water within that we store in our own bodies.

When we talk about all our relations, we are talking about being related to everything in creation. We honor all our relations, and all the living beings found in the east, south, west, and the north directions. That includes our relations found above our N'ku'set Grandfather Sun, Tepkunset Grandmother Moon, to the clouds, and to the Star Beings. We honor all our relations below us that exist within Wksitqamuk Mother Earth. We honor those that live in the air, among the earth, and underground. We honor those that live within the water, and the ones that have deep roots that grow within Mother Earth herself.

We honor our Ancestors by acknowledging the seven generations that have walked before us and who continue to guide us along our path. It is through honoring ourselves and being aligned with our spiritual path that we in turn can honor the next seven generations that will follow us.

The Seven Sacred Grandfather Teachings

The Seven Sacred Grandfather teachings lay out a cultural foundation and show us the moral stepping stones that we must walk to live a good and happy life. Each lesson— love, respect, courage, humility, honesty, wisdom, and truth—work together and outline how each person should conduct themselves and live their life accordingly. Each is interconnected and works cooperatively with one another, and it is by fully embracing each of the Seven Sacred Grandfather teachings separately that those teachings all come together and work in harmony.

I am grateful for my Mi'kmaq culture and for the teachings I have learned through my journey in life. I have always had a strong connection to the natural and spiritual world, and although these teachings aren't something I grew up with, since I was raised in the Catholic Church, and had only occasional visits with my Newfoundland grandmother as a child, it was as I became an adult and started my work as a spirit talker that I began to learn more about my own culture.

Fortunately, over the years different teachers have shared their wisdom and knowledge with me, and I'm deeply appreciative to gain those teachings. However, I'm still learning and by no means am an Elder. Being a proud Mi'kmaq person, I pull on those traditions in my own life and apply these principles to help other people as well, with the most fundamental aspect of these practices being the expression of love and gratitude.

The Drum

For centuries Indigenous people have found a connection to the sound of the drum and to the beating of the heart. The belief is that both share a similar purpose: to provide life through that beat, which serves to help create oneness between people and nature. The drum has a spirit all on its own—with the hoop representing the circle of life and the drumbeat representing the heartbeat of Mother Earth.

She is a mother to all living things in our world, and in the same way our own mother gives us life, Mother Earth gives life to all creation. She teaches us the importance of protecting the land and, most importantly, our waterways, because they are the lifeblood that sustains our world.

Her heartbeat has been embedded within our own chest so we will not forget, and it is through the action of drumming that we acknowledge we are her children. Many ceremonial songs include the beat of the drum, and one of my favorites is "The Honor Song." The drum is a connection that allows us to send our message back to Mother Earth, to let her know that we hear her, and that we see her, and that we thank her for giving us life. It is through that action and the beat that we promote love and respect for all living things and this connects us to the earth and the ground we walk upon.

The Four Sacred Medicines

Within Indigenous culture there's always some sort of thanks given, and the Mi'kmaq word for "thank you" is Wela'lin. We thank the Creator Kisu'lk, we thank Grandfather Sun, we thank Mother Earth, and we thank all the species on the earth through our interactions with them. When you take the life of a tree to make a canoe, you thank the tree; when you take the life of an animal to nourish yourself, you thank that animal. Traditionally, the offering of Tobacco is used in these moments because it is the most sacred medicine used for ceremonial offerings within Mi'kmaq culture.

Tobacco is connected to the east, which is where the sun rises each day, and is considered the first medicine to be gifted to the inhabitants of Turtle Island. Tobacco is used through non-smoke offerings, so that when you take something from Mother Earth or offer prayers you do so with gratitude and thanks. It is considered the most sacred of the four medicines and is a direct link to the Creator.

Within the western direction of the medicine wheel, Sage is found, and it is known for its antiseptic properties and its ability to energetically cleanse an object or space. It has an unmistakable scent, and its sacred smoke is known to spiritually purify and cleanse an area.

Cedar is often utilized in sweat lodge ceremonies for safety and protection of the ceremony itself. It is helpful for soothing a troubled heart because of its lush green color and its connection to the heart chakra. It occupies the south direction of the medicine wheel and is connected to deep spiritual healing.

The fourth sacred medicine is Sweetgrass, which is also known as "mother's hair," and is found in the north direction of the medicine wheel. Sweetgrass has an unmistakable sweet scent, and ceremony is heavily involved in its collection, and through the process of braiding the individual blades of grass.

I feel strongly connected to the sacredness of Sweetgrass and love the amount of care that goes into the whole process: finding the plants, speaking prayers while picking the medicine, and carefully ensuring that future generations will have access to it by protecting the roots of the plants themselves.

I love that prayers are also spoken while it is being braided and how important it is that when two or more people come together to speak a prayer that it strengthens those intentions. With Sweetgrass one person speaks prayers and braids the grass while the other person holds the other end and prays for the other person's prayers to be heard. Sweetgrass is important to the work that I do and is a bridge to the spirit world and a way of strengthening the connection to the Ancestors through the smudging process.

These four sacred medicines can be used in conjunction with each other through the act of smudging. It is important to remember that smudging has no power until you create the ceremony through your words and actions. It's about the energy you put into it and the intentions behind your words. If you smudge and you speak with fear or anger, then it ruins its effect and you won't be able to tap into its intended purpose. So, it's important to ensure that you are in a good headspace and mindset when smudging. Also, when a woman is on her moon time, traditionally she is not to smudge or touch any medicines. The woman's body is in a state of cleansing, and the power of that cleansing can actually reduce the effectiveness of the medicines. Sacred items should also not be touched for four days after consuming alcohol.

USING THE SACRED MEDICINES

Smudging has become an integral part of my life and in the work that I do. The use of sacred smoke isn't connected to a singular belief or tradition, but within my culture there are four sacred medicines that are incorporated into ceremonies. Each of these medicines offer their own unique energy and are located within the four directions of the medicine wheel.

You might find sacred herbs connected to your own faith or cultural traditions to be useful smudging tools and resins, such as frankincense, myrrh, and copal. Sacred bits of wood like sandalwood and palo santo and even flowers including roses or lavender can be powerful sources of spiritual protection.

You can place the four sacred medicines within a piece of pottery or a shell, but just ensure that you use something of the earth. You can light the medicines, preferably with matches, and blow out the flame once it has begun to smolder. Start by expressing gratitude to the masculine and feminine aspects of the Creator for your many blessings in life and then allow the smoke to move gently over your hands and to spiritually cleanse you.

Cup the smoke into your hands and pull it over your head, then ask for the Great Spirit to help you know the truth and to know good things. Continue to pull the smoke into your closed eyes and ask to see the truth and to see good things. Pull the smoke into each ear and ask to hear the truth and good things. Move the smoke toward your mouth and ask to speak the truth and good things. Pull the smoke toward your heart and ask for the Creator to help you feel the truth and feel good things. Finally, sweep the smoke over your body and cleanse yourself, including your arms and legs.

Respect for Tradition

Learning the cultural practice of smudging can be of great benefit to anyone, but just like any other Indigenous ceremony or custom, such as the Pipe Ceremony, the Sweat Lodge, the Vision Quest, the Naming Ceremony, and the Talking Circle, the process should be taught by a trained Elder. My cultural traditions run deep and contain significant universal truths, but it's important to remember that respect should be given to these teachings, and that the practice should not be changed. If you are taught a certain way by an Elder, don't take the teaching and try to make it your own by changing the practice. Respect the teaching in its totality and respect the way it was taught to you.

I have been fortunate to be the recipient of many teachings in life, and I've had many teachers. There have been many knowledgable men and women who have crossed my path, especially within the Mi'kmaq culture, who have taught me lessons that have enriched my experiences, my life, and have helped me reconnect to my culture.

Being an Indigenous person and reclaiming parts of myself by learning more about my culture has strengthened my innate feelings about how important and essential it is to work together within the human nation. It's about how we treat those around us that matters, and by showing compassion and love for your fellow brothers and sisters, your aunts and uncles, your mothers and fathers, your grandmothers and grandfathers, your cousins, and friends, true peace can occur. We should all work together and care for one another and recognize that we are all one, we are all part of the same family.

I'd like to end this chapter with a prayer I've written. I sincerely hope that you make it, and the concepts within, part of your own life and spiritual practice. Each one of us is always creating our own realities and our own lives in this circle of life together: co-existing, co-dependent, co-creating our destinies. In all seven directions, I thank you. All of us are one with the Great Spirit, Wela'lin. Thank you for our many lives, and the love and light we share. You are all my relatives. You are all my relations. Mist No'kmaq.

MI'KMAQ PRAYER

Msit No'kmaq, all my relations. I honor you in the circle of life today. I am grateful to acknowledge you in this prayer.

Kisu'lk, Creator, for the ultimate gift of life: wela'lin, thank you.

Nisgam, Grandfather Sun, for the ultimate gift of my spirit and my shadow: wela'lin, thank you.

Ogijinew, Mother Earth, for the mineral nation, which has built my body and maintained my bones and all foundations of my physical life and experience: wela'lin, thank you.

To the Plant Nation, which sustains my organs, my body, and gives me healing herbs for sickness: wela'lin, thank you.

To the Animal Nation, which feeds me and offers me companionship in this walk of life: wela'lin, thank you.

To Osgijinew, the people who share my path upon the sacred wheel of this earthly life: wela'lin, thank you my brothers and sisters.

To the Spirit Nation, which guides me through the ups and downs and shows me the light in everything through it all: wela'lin, thank you.

In all seven directions, thank you. You are all my relations, my relatives, and without whom I would not live. We are in the circle of life together, co-existing, co-dependent, co-creating our destiny. We are one nation evolving from the other, and yet dependent on the Great Spirit and the universe above and the Mother Earth below. I honor myself and my spirit in all four directions: east, south, west, north.

All of us are one with you, Great Spirit.

Wela'lin, thank you for our lives and the love and light that we share.

Msit No'kmaq, all my relations.

CHAPTER 31

KLUSUWAQNN NA MELKIKNAQ+L

WORDS HAVE POWER

If you are reading this book, it's more than likely you have an interest in the spirit world and wish to become a more spiritually connected person. We are all meant to progress, learn, grow, and connect to one another during our many lifetimes. What we experience in the physical world is temporary, but the lessons we learn are ones we take with us lifetime after lifetime. I have consciously chosen to be a student of life and allow Spirit to guide me. I see the wisdom I have gained to be knowledge that is meant to be shared with others, and the spiritual practices I have incorporated into my life have helped deepen my connection to the spirit world.

Depending on your upbringing and experiences, you might have deep-seated notions of what prayer is and how to pray. I have found that it's common for people to utilize prayer almost as a vehicle of panicked requests to the Creator, and do so in moments of duress, but they often don't really give it much thought otherwise. Part of becoming more connected and being open to receiving messages from Spirit stems from having a good dialogue with the spirit world.

Speaking prayerful words out loud enhances your intentions. When we speak our words it not only amplifies the sound of our request through our voices, but it strengthens our words through the conviction we use. It's important to not only be mindful of the words you choose to speak, but also to consider the energy of your words themselves.

If you are in an angry frame of mind, or are speaking to Spirit out of fear or frustration, it will impact what you are trying to convey and will lessen the effectiveness of the prayerful words themselves. If you say something with uncertainty or are struggling with a health concern and continually speak to Spirit from a place of fear, your worries can impact the effectiveness of the prayer you wish to be answered. Instead, it is ideal to come from a place of inner knowing that divine will is at play; just remove all expectations of what the result will be and trust that you will be okay regardless of the outcome.

Imagining the following two situations in your mind might help solidify this concept a bit more. For example, a person is struggling with a major health concern and is uncertain about their future or what their long-term prognosis will be. They might wake up every morning angry at the world and the Creator. This is a valid emotional response, but it is also a choice. They may continually focus on the setbacks they are facing and dwell on what might potentially happen rather than empowering a positive outcome.

In the second scenario the same person is given the same diagnosis, but rather than choosing to wake up angry and focus on their fears, they consciously decide to pray and use words with the belief that they can be healed. They choose to believe that miracles are real and that divine timing is chosen by a force that has a much greater scope for where our lives are headed.

Even on an energetic level the second scenario feels lighter and more at peace with the outcome. There is hopefulness and optimism. There is a certainty that healing is possible, but an understanding that ultimately our life charts are created long before our present incarnations.

By letting go of expectations and releasing the need to control the situation, it can positively impact the energy we infuse into the words of our prayers. A person may obsessively pray for resolution, not realizing that by rehashing their concerns it is like reopening energetic wounds that can delay the healing process.

Most of the time this is easier said than done. It can be extremely difficult to understand the divine will of the universe, but by focusing on the words you speak, and the energy you infuse into your intentions, you can move through life with more ease. By knowing that you can manifest a more peaceful existence for yourself you can greatly impact the world around you. It all starts on an individual level, but our thoughts create our realities, and it's important to even be mindful of how we think.

It is also equally important to call in your whole spirit team when asking for assistance from the universe. When you address your spirit guides, angels, spirit totem animal, power animals, and Ancestors, their presence can also strengthen the power behind your words and actions. Knowing your spirit totem animal and power animal and invoking their spiritual medicine they exhibit, which can easily be researched, can also be helpful. For instance, the ferocity of my power animal, the polar bear, protects me while the eagle assists in my spiritual work. You want to call in as much love and healing as you can, and it's always a good practice to include others in your prayerful words.

The concept that there is strength in numbers also pertains to your people in Spirit, and why prayer circles can be incredibly healing. Within my own spirit talker tribe course, I encourage my students who are struggling to pray for one another and to actively ask for prayers when needed. I've heard of many instances where people have been positively impacted by the healing effects of my tribe, and I have even felt the effects of that divine power firsthand.

When you speak your words to the Creator, there is an assumed level of confidentiality that takes place while you request your prayers to be heard. It is almost as if a cone of silence is placed above you that funnels your words directly to the Creator. I strongly recommend including all your connections to the other side, and give your spirit team permission, so that they are privy to the conversation and are allowed to intervene if they can do so. When you include their assistance and their positive influence behind your words it will only enhance the intentions of your prayers.

Prayer consists simply of the words you exchange with the entirety of the spirit world. It is not remembering a specific line or passage from any book. It is your conversation with the Creator, guides, angels, totem animals, Ancestors. Speak out loud and be clear with your thoughts, words, and actions, and have daily conversations. Words are powerful, so speak them intentionally, with unconditional love, and never think for a second you are not being heard. It all begins with your prayerful words. This is the first step of Spirit communication.

HOW TO CONDUCT YOUR OWN PRAYER

When you start a prayer always think of who you wish to address the prayer to. Here are a few examples:

Great Spirit, Creator, hear my words and heart.

My spirit guides, hear my words. I need your help.

My Ancestors in the spirit world, hear my words.

Then, speak your intention. Here are a few examples:

I am giving a speech today and will require your love, light, and grace. Help me be present and inspired with the message I wish to share.

I am changing careers and feel a bit confused as to what direction I need to go. I ask for you to make it abundantly clear the direction that is in alignment with my highest purpose.

I ask that you be with me today and help me be more aware of unconditional love.

Finally, end your prayer. Here are a few examples:

Sealed in faith, trust, and truth, I confirm this with my entire being.

With thanks and gratitude—all my relations.

Or just end it with "*all my relations.*"

Remember to speak out loud, clearly, and with all your heart!

CHAPTER 32

ELTASIK T+L PISKWITA'TAL

CREATE SPACE TO RECEIVE

Meditation has been proven to have significant benefits for one's overall health and well-being—from lowering anxiety levels to becoming more focused and present to raising one's vibration.

Prayerful words and meditation are necessary cornerstones for deepening a spiritual connection. By combining both practices you can have a two-way conversation with the spirit world. It is my belief that prayerful words are essential for communicating with the other side, and it's where you speak your intentions to Spirit. Meditation helps to quiet the mind, which creates space for spirit messages to be received. It will help you be still and mindful so that you can receive messages, and it will also help you find presence and balance within your life. Too many people are overburdened by their thoughts—and the perceived thoughts of others—making it difficult to move beyond those thoughts.

I encourage you to incorporate prayerful words and meditation into your daily life because of its profound impact on your spiritual connection. This is especially true if you desire to have a deeper connection to the Creator and all spirit people. If your intention is to have a relationship with Spirit and if you trust in the process, you will undoubtedly begin to see results. When you meditate daily and become more mindful within your life, you will see extensive changes in your ability to connect as well.

If you don't know how to meditate and create space within your mind, your thoughts may run rampant and cloud your ability to receive messages from the spirit world. Spirit won't be able to get past the mental mind noise in your head to relay messages to you. You will need to remember and relearn how to create small moments of space within your mind.

We were all born with this ability but have been conditioned by our earthly environment and experience to forget the stillness and mindfulness that exists within. We have been taught to be, feel, think, and do, but not to be mindfully quiet and still within our own thoughts.

I suggest that you begin a practice of creating space within your mind through meditation. This can be done for short periods of time every day—not for hours on end, as you may have heard. Meditation is an exercise and requires practice; perhaps you can be mindfully present for only 10 seconds on your first attempt. Your second attempt may last 15 seconds, and so on. Start small and increase in small increments to build a healthy habit. Like any other physical exercise you do often, your ability to go beyond yesterday's limits will increase, but just a little at a time. Finally, if you say you can't do it, you are right. Why? Because that is the reality you have chosen to create.

There are different types of meditation exercises you can do daily, even if it is just for a few minutes. The first is mindfulness meditation with your eyes closed. For this, sit or lie down, be still, and focus on your breath. Choose to just be present and feel where you physically are. Focus on your breath, which is slow and rhythmic. If you notice a thought of the past or potential future, choose to let it go and refocus on your breath. This type of meditation is very useful when you are going through a situation that may bring about anxiety. When you move into the still-ness and presence, you are more in alignment with all of creation. By choosing to move into this space within your mind, it allows you to surrender and let Spirit realign your energy to your purpose.

The next type of meditation I recommend you practice is mindful meditation with eyes open, then closed. With your eyes open, find a focal point, such as a crystal, plant, or even by staring outside a window. Focus your attention but allow the mind to be still, again focusing on your breath. After a few minutes, close your eyes and begin to meditate mindfully with your eyes closed, following the approach I described above. This time, close your eyes and picture what you were just looking at. Re-create that same image within your mind with as much detail as possible, and breathe.

The last type of meditation I suggest incorporating into your life is a visualization meditation on a specific place. This should be a place you can mentally return to at will. I suggest a place you cherish in the physical world and have personally been to, like an oceanside beach or a special spot in the forest. Imagine yourself there and incorporate as much of your spiritual senses as you can while you are in this state—what the air feels like, what sounds you remember, and even just the way you feel when you're in that environment. Whatever spot you choose, try to choose a peaceful location where you can rest in pleasant solitude. This type of meditation is great in combination with the others, but it is also helpful in stressful moments when you need to mentally be somewhere else for a moment.

You will need to spend only a few minutes on each type of meditation, and there is no need to use a timer unless you feel called to do so; your mind and body will know when it's time to transition out of meditation. I would suggest spending about three minutes a day on each of these techniques I shared with you, and it won't be long before you start to notice a difference within yourself and in how you connect with the world around you.

These three meditation practices can help you develop your psychic abilities and work on the area responsible for creating mental space for psychic work. They are also helpful at increasing clairvoyant impressions and training your brain to allow spirit-initiated messages to be received. It's about stillness, because when we pray, we *speak* our truth, but when we meditate, we sit in silence and wait to *receive* truth.

As you continue this journey and become more open to receive, Spirit will speak to you in mental visual flashes and sometimes symbols that are specific to you, and it will provide you with the tools to understand this intuitive language for yourself. Your very own language of Spirit.

The mindful eyes-open technique is essential for this. With practice, you will notice that psychic impressions begin to appear to you spontaneously, even when your eyes are open. Our minds can see more than we realize, and we see our physical reality but can also see psychically at the same time. An image may suddenly come into your mental awareness without you actively seeking it out. You could be at work staring at your computer screen or talking to a friend, when suddenly you see yourself in a completely different setting, or perhaps a symbol will come to mind.

As you become more focused on presence, you will notice that the senses the Elders relied on for survival will strengthen within yourself. The psychic muscles we are all born with but that have atrophied through living in a physical reality will become stronger. My experience has taught me that through reconnection, prayerful words, and presence, we can deepen our relationship to the natural and spiritual world. Each of us can develop a stronger level of intuition and will be more connected to universal wisdom.

CHAPTER 33

KLE'LWE'TUWO'TMKEWEY

CLAIRSENTIENCE

We are never alone, and Spirit is always communicating with us. Most people either don't realize the signs, or don't remember when they receive messages from their loved ones. But remember, this is not an exclusive ability; it is a divine universal language we all have access to, and anyone can learn. Every person can connect, though how a message is received may vary. We are all born psychic and connected to the spirit world. The more you work with these spiritual tools, the more profound your experiences will become.

Our loved ones in the spirit world find different ways to communicate to spirit talkers. So that we can effectively provide healing messages, it's essential to understand how that communication works and learn how to translate those messages properly.

One way Spirit may communicate with us is through clairsentience: a psychic impression of "clear feeling." It is a great way of tuning in to those energetic messages received from Spirit and figuring out the meaning behind the message. There are other means of receiving messages from Spirit, which are commonly referred to as the "Clairs": clairsentience, clairaudience, claircognizance, clairalience, and clairgustance. They often work in relation to one another, but I use clairsentience in my work to add depth and specificity to the other spirit messages I receive.

When we think about intuition—your inner knowing—or having a gut feeling, it's about having a clear sense or feeling about something. Psychically, clairsentience is about an emotional awareness and perceiving messages in a different way. Instead of receiving auditory sounds or visual images, you would pick up on impressions either from a location, a living person, or from someone in Spirit; these different aspects of clairsentience provide us with different forms of information. So, as you work on strengthening your intuitive abilities, you are learning and building upon your internal psychic knowledge.

Intuition is an ability and a skill that is constantly growing and evolving; it is not a static thing. It isn't something you can ever fully have or possess; rather, you are continually learning and expanding upon your intuitive knowledge. Think of it as school (the "tuition" in "intuition") that never ends because we are all spirits having a human experience. As such, we are always learning and expanding through this life and our many other lifetimes. As our psychic abilities grow, we also grow as people.

A common example many have encountered in their life is physically feeling the energy that exists within certain locations. It could be an imprint left there from the past that you notice when you walk into a space. You might walk into a department store and suddenly feel tired, drained, or weighed down. You could feel exhausted when you walk out because there's an energy imprint of other people feeling frustrated or unhappy. As you walk through that space, your aura will interact with those energetic imprints, and it will influence you.

This is especially true for people who are empathetic or very clairsentient because they sense Spirit on a much deeper level. In that sense, they tend to notice when their energetic batteries become drained much more quickly when they have not properly protected or grounded themselves by smudging or clearing their auras. Occasionally clearing your aura to maintain a good balance in life is good, but the reality is that maintaining balance and having the ability to create energetic boundaries is essential for spiritual growth.

When interacting or connecting to a person in the physical world, sometimes you might feel their energy. Oftentimes people are empaths or clairsentient without even realizing it, and it's by feeling energies that are not our own that we realize how much energy we pick up from the people in our surroundings. When we receive psychic impressions from living people or Spirit, rather than from a place, there is a distinction in the way we can receive those messages. There is also a difference between psychics and mediums and how they receive their messages.

All spirit talkers are psychic and possess the ability to "vibe out" a living person and receive messages from their deceased loved ones, but not all psychics are mediums, meaning they can communicate directly with spirits. So, when you are tuning into a living person's energy, and their aura, you are doing so by picking up on that information psychically. That is the easiest way to explain the difference between a psychic and a medium, and even though a psychic might receive some information from the other side, most of the information comes from the person they are reading themselves and their aura.

When you're "vibing out" a person's aura, feel their energy and receive information about their life in a psychic sense, so you can help guide them. When you connect to somebody in Spirit it's a different level of energy that you're tapping into and feels different in a very subtle way. In the same way we can be impacted by a place and the energetic imprint that exists there, we can also be impacted by the vibes we pick up from other people.

Sometimes you can instantly know if someone is having a good day or is upset about something, if they dislike you or enjoy your energy, or if they've been depressed. Everyone carries energy with them, and you can pick up on aspects of their personality from their vibration alone. Even without knowing much about them you might get a sense of what type of person they are, what makes them tick, and what makes them excited about life.

This is all based on what you tune in to on a clairsentient level. You might have even looked back at your life and thought about your own experiences when you felt something about a person you didn't know very well and found out later that you were correct.

There are ways of enhancing clairsentient abilities by working with them. I recommend that people practice by tuning in to the vibrations of a stranger or a friend of a friend. You can pray to the Creator that someone who is open-minded be available to practice on. Then prior to meeting with them be sure to smudge yourself, pray, and meditate.

Be honest and tell the person that you are just learning and want to practice on what you pick up through clairsentience and try to tune in to your own body and see what you pick up on from their body. You might feel knee pain, which may correspond to a past injury they've experienced, or can tell they suffer from migraines. You might feel sadness from them or excitement. Consciously tune in and discover what information you feel about the person's past, present, and potential future. Relay the messages to them, and follow the bread crumbs.

During season one of *Spirit Talker*, we filmed an episode in Halifax, Nova Scotia. There are no reserves within the city to serve the large Indigenous population that is scattered throughout the municipality, so the Halifax Native Friendship Center acts as a cultural hub for the community.

While we were filming, I spoke with Elder Debbie Eisan as she helped me put ribbons onto a ceremonial shirt. It is a traditional shirt sometimes worn by Indigenous people in ceremonies, and it is what I wear onstage during my live events and on the TV series itself. The ribbons represent the certain colors associated with an individual, and each ribbon tells a story. On my shirt, I wear the four directional colors: yellow, red, black, white.

As we were finishing up filming for the day, we got up to hug each other, and I immediately felt a pain on the right side of my head. It felt like the pain you would expect from a stroke, and it was so intense I could feel a cut from a surgical knife subtly upon my own head. It was a very momentary pain and lasted only a few seconds, but it was strong enough to make me aware.

When I tapped into this woman's aura it hit me like a ton of bricks, and I had to move away from her so the pain would subside, and when I did it stopped immediately. I asked her, "Has anybody you've known had a stroke or brain issue?" She told me that she had a brain tumor in 2011 the size of a golf ball, which had to be surgically removed. After she explained this to me, she lifted her hair up to show me the scar.

The illness she experienced had created an immense fear in her life to the point that she had obsessed about it coming back, and every time she would have a headache her mind would instantly assume the worst. So why would I be able to feel this energy from her? Why did I feel her pain in that moment? There was obviously a reason for me to have that experience, and it's the same reason empaths feel so deeply, and why people who have strong clairsentient abilities can be so sensitive to the energy of other people.

I later understood that I was meant to assist her that day in moving forward in life without fear. The intention for becoming a more spiritually enlightened person, for nurturing your psychic growth, should be that you have a desire to help people through their journey in life. It isn't about serving our own ego and about wanting to be the best; rather, it's about helping others move through life with more ease, since disease creates illness within the body. We should just want to offset the struggles people face by providing healing in a balanced and appropriate way without draining ourselves in the process.

When we pick up clairsentient messages from Spirit, they can come through in a similar way that we would feel from a living person. Instead of tuning in to that person's body, we attempt to connect to their loved ones in Spirit.

If you can, try this for the first time with the same person with whom you did the other exercise.

Prior to meeting with them smudge yourself with medicine that has special meaning to you, pray, and meditate. I personally always use Sweetgrass when inviting a spirit to connect to me because of its connection to the Ancestors. Then light the medicine inside your smudge shell and invite the spirits to connect with you. I offer smoke to the spirits as an invitation to provide messages and give them permission to stay there until the sitter leaves.

Remind the sitter that you are just learning and want to practice your ability to feel things from people in the spirit world and try to tune in to what messages are presented to you. I find that most people are typically stronger in one of the "Clairs," and you might find you receive visual impressions or auditory ones, rather than feeling the energy. Whatever the case, they often work in conjunction with one another, and the purpose is to practice and invite Spirit to assist you in the process.

During the final episode of season one of *Spirit Talker*, I spoke to a woman in Millbrook First Nation whose mother was deaf since birth. I could feel my ears being clogged almost like they were filled with water, and I wasn't able to hear clearly. This woman was named Mary, and she was a great communicator, and came through strongly. I feel her physical limitation of being deaf forced her to become a clear communicator in other ways in life, which even carried over into how she communicates in Spirit.

What people may not know is that the desire Spirit has to communicate with us is just as strong as the desire we have to communicate with them. Our loved ones in Spirit will often relay messages to spirit talkers through clairsentience because it is a great indicator of who they were in life. Relaying information about aspects of themselves is a way of validating that it's actually them coming through. This is exactly what Mary did when she relayed that information about her deafness to me. Spirit is often waiting for a moment to grasp on to so they can speak to us, and whether it's through a spirit talker like myself, or through some other synchronistic event or sign, they will try to make a connection. The truth is, though, that nobody needs an outside person to have a continued relationship to their loved ones.

Becoming more in tune with your own clairsentient ability can be immensely helpful in healing others as well as yourself. If you struggle with feeling drained by the energy of others, or take on their burdens, it's essential to know where your energy ends and another's begins. By creating healthy energetic boundaries, your ability to help others and yourself becomes so much less burdensome, and even more rewarding. It is when we know how and when to help that we can do the best in this world.

By being more open to receive and coming from a grounded place, your ability to communicate and understand the universal language of Spirit will become clearer. If you are interested in allowing more spirit messages into your life, I suggest that you establish a rapport with the spirit world. Let them know you are open and available to receive messages from people in the light. Invite and allow the spirit world to send you signs and information and be prepared to receive the messages they have for you. Completely let go of the expectation of how that information should come to you and work with what flows into your awareness.

A SENSING AND FEELING
EXERCISE FOR CLAIRSENTIENCE

Ask a friend or family member to let you hold a picture or object that belonged to someone they know well but whom you have never met.

Mindfully hold the picture or object and stare at it for a few minutes. Allow your psychic sense to vibe it out and feel personality traits of the person. Did they feel happy? Sad? Alive or passed? How old do they feel to you? Do you feel or sense anything upon your body when holding it? Perhaps they had bad legs and couldn't walk, and you are feeling an aching in one or more of your legs. Be very mindful and aware of your own body and personality traits when you do this exercise, as it will reveal much psychic information.

Share your findings with your friend or family member and validate your impressions.

CHAPTER 34

KLE'LNE'TAPTM~KEWEY
CLAIRVOYANCE

During the filming of my first season of *Spirit Talker* I visited Wagmatcook First Nation, which is nestled along the Bras d'Or Lake and lies within the heart of Cape Breton Island. Cape Breton makes up a large portion of my province, both geographically and culturally speaking, and while I was in the community of Wagmatcook, I visited the Elder's Center where cultural traditions are still going strong. It is here where I learned about the game of Waltes, a tradition that existed long before European contact, and its significance to Mi'kmaq culture.

It is played with two players taking turns hitting a concave wooden bowl against a table while six two-sided dice are inside, which causes the pieces to randomly land either upright or facedown inside the bowl. There are 51 counting sticks awarded for each die that lands faceup, and there is one kingpin shaped like the forward half of an arrow and three notched sticks representing the other. The kingpin is called the old man, or kesegoo, and the notched sticks were his three wives, and the plain sticks were his children. When you play the game you fan your hand over the dice, since this gesture is meant to make them dance and roll in your favor. The game can be played round after round and can even go on indefinitely. It is fun, fast-paced, and believed to be a favorite within the spirit world itself.

My reason for writing about the game of Waltes isn't to explain the rules or to go into depth about its historical importance—although I am happy to say it has had a resurgence in recent years, with more Indigenous people seeking out traditional customs as a way of reclaiming their roots. Instead, I want to talk about what our Elders did back in the day with the game and how spiritually significant it was to our people.

The bowls had a dual purpose: they weren't just used for the game, they were used in ceremonies as spiritual tools. Even the maple trees that were used to create these bowls came from the forest, and as such were infused with the positive and sacred energy that can be found among the trees. The interconnectedness of culture, daily life, and spiritual practice is found throughout Indigenous teachings. So, it is not a surprise to me how a game could also be a profoundly spiritual tool for connecting to the Divine.

The bowls would be filled with water and left outside under the moonlight during the four nights that surround a full moon. After those four nights had passed, my Ancestors would smudge and pray, and then the ceremony would begin. An Elder would gaze blankly into the bowl, which would produce visions and create inner visual insights within their own mind's eye. They would provide insight on where to hunt or camp, what medicine should be picked to heal the sick, and contain any other answers the Ancestors could provide from the spirit world.

In this sense, they would be able to clearly see past the veil of the spirit world; in the modern sense, they would be considered a clairvoyant. The terms psychic, clairvoyant, and seer have existed for eons, long before we even had the language to describe what they were. Unfortunately, throughout history those in power deemed certain cultural practices, spiritual beliefs, and being a spirit talker as unholy acts; to this day many people struggle with connecting to Spirit because of the limitations the church had instilled in them early in life.

European colonists, especially church officials such as the Jesuit or Catholic priests, wanted to strip away the culture from Indigenous people. They saw what the Elders were able to do and mistook our beliefs as something that wasn't to be trusted. Because of that, they drilled holes in the Waltes bowls so that they could no longer hold water. Even today you may find some people who still have their ancestor's bowls that have been passed down from generation to generation, and there are holes drilled into the bottom of them.

Church officials believed that they could take away the ability to see from my Ancestors, the Mi'kmaq people, and all Indigenous people of this land. Their intention for drilling these holes was to ruin the ceremony. The church thought that if the ceremony didn't exist, the Elders would lose that ability to seek guidance from the spirit world, which in their eyes did not come from the same source as their own religious beliefs.

All Indigenous cultures have ceremonies, for renewal, for rebirth, for healing, for celebrations. Similar to the game of Waltes, our pipe ceremonies are sacred and are used as a way of speaking to spirits and to offer prayers directly to the Creator. The role of a Pipe Carrier is one a person is born into and requires immense responsibility, and it is a calling not to be taken lightly.

The smoke carries the prayers up to the Creator, but the reality is if you take away the ceremony it does not mean that you can't pray and that those prayers won't be heard. The same is true if you take away the Waltes bowl; you can still see in a spiritual sense, and although it is considered a sacred object and connected to ceremony, it is ultimately a tool. Although spiritual tools can assist us and empower our own personal connection to the spirit world, they do not create the abilities themselves.

Key to connecting with the spirit world is the opening of the mind. When I connect to Spirit I am staring blankly, but I am mentally in the zone; I am in the space to receive messages from Spirit, and the reason is to reconnect to that gap space within my mind and to that void.

This idea is closely related to being in a meditative state, and it's about being truly present and being open to receive messages from Spirit. When my mind is in this space where I allow myself to receive messages from Spirit, and where those subtle flashes of information come into my mind, I pay extra attention.

I am aware of what I'm seeing, which can sometimes be literal or figurative, and it's about tuning in to the images that you see to try and understand the difference. It's important to touch on how to develop your clairvoyant abilities specifically, which can be done through a strong practice of visualized meditation. It is through consistent meditation, visualized meditation, and by training your mind to hold on to an image within the mind itself that you can increase and strengthen this ability.

A good and simple way to practice is to hold on to a clear quartz crystal in your right hand and examine it closely, and really study it. Then take that crystal away, but still visualize it and all its minute details, the color, the shape, even its texture. By taking it all in, you are exercising that muscle within your own mind to see more clearly in a psychic sense. When you visualize something in your mind's eye, you are choosing to bring that idea into your awareness.

I don't like using the word imagination when it comes to clairvoyance because it's easy for people to assume what they are seeing isn't real, or they may feel the need to try and rationalize away a sign from Spirit because they don't trust their abilities. I choose to rephrase the word to "image-ination" because it is through your ability to *initiate* an image within your own mind that you can see it. When Spirit inserts an image into your mind that you were not expecting, they are literally putting that image into your awareness. When you create mental space for images to come in and bring yourself to a mindful state, that form of spirit communication is possible.

When you invite Spirit in and create a space within yourself to receive, you will notice subtle images from them more and more. When speaking from a place of truth, integrity, honesty, and compassion, and by presenting these messages with the utmost sense of unconditional love, there will be a shift in your consciousness.

You will realize that these seemingly random images will mean something to someone. That the person you're sitting next to or who you're speaking with will understand the meaning of the message. Just remember to trust in Spirit, and trust in your own abilities. The messages you will receive from Spirit come from a pure and sacred place and can provide so much healing. So when you train your mind through the process of creating and holding space for those images to appear, you are creating the possibility within your mind to remember how to see.

Seeing is believing, and I know when you work at holding images in your mind, you will strengthen your mind muscle, one that has long atrophied. The secret to receiving messages from the spirit world clairvoyantly is to allow your mind to be mindful and open for small moments of time. If you never create moments of space to receive, how will you ever feel, see, or hear what Spirit has been trying to communicate to you?

PRACTICE YOUR CLAIRVOYANCE

For this exercise it is important that you have practiced the three exercises in the "Create Space to Receive" chapter.

Do this exercise with a trusted friend or family member who is open to your development, if possible.

Get yourself a pottery bowl or a wooden bowl or even a large glass and fill it with water.

Say a prayer you have written ("Words have power" exercise) and invite your Ancestors, guides, and angels to help you clairvoyantly receive a visual impression in relation to guiding someone with a clairvoyant visual message or connecting to your friends' loved ones through clairvoyant impressions.

Gaze into the water mindfully—be present and mentally observe any images that may come into your mind's eye. See with your spirit eyes and internal vision, and this can take place only when you are mindfully aware. It may be a literal clairvoyant message or it may be a figurative clairvoyant message; either way trust and work with what you receive. It may come in bits and pieces, or you may get a lot at once; every person is different.

Whatever comes to you, do your best to validate and continue the process until you feel the message is complete.

Thank who you feel the message came from and stop mindfully focusing on your water and thank your friend for being open to the process.

CHAPTER 35

KLE'LNE'TASTASIKEWEY
CLAIRAUDIENCE

Throughout my life I have been blessed with the ability to understand the language of Spirit and have become more attuned with the messages that I receive. This has allowed me to assist others in learning this energetic language, so that they can help themselves and the people within their own lives become more enlightened and fully grasp that we are all spirits having a human experience.

One important aspect of spirit communication centers around the concept of "clear hearing," which is also known as clairaudience. This form of extrasensory perception was the first psychic ability I was able to manifest when I began doing this work, when I began to clearly hear names inside my head without bringing them into my own awareness. Whenever I heard a name, I didn't understand why I was hearing it but I trusted that I was hearing *something*. Because of that trust, I have become more open and able to receive messages from Spirit in this way. Since then, I have worked to develop this gift, and nurtured my spiritual growth, and become a stronger spirit talker because I devote so much of myself to the process.

From my own experience I hear Spirit in two different ways: in my mind, or from outside myself. Typically, when I hear a voice in my mind this comes from spirits on the other side who are communicating with me from the light. That doesn't mean that they won't speak out loud sometimes, because they do, but in my experience hearing an audible voice typically comes from an earthbound spirit.

When I do hear earthbound spirits, they are an outside entity literally speaking to me, as opposed to spirits who are in the light who operate at a higher energetic level and can communicate through their thoughts alone. I encounter more clairaudient messages in my mind than outside of myself because I actively connect to people's loved ones. By doing this work, I have found the ability of clear hearing to be the most helpful to validate the presence of a loved one in Spirit.

When spirits communicate with us through clairaudience it isn't through long-winded speeches; it's typically a quick little burst of audible voices or thoughts. It may be a name, a date, or a meaningful word, and as you practice you will learn to discern the sound of your own mental voice from those in Spirit. I like to think of the voice of Spirit as a quieter, smaller voice behind my own that wants to guide us in some way or draw our attention to something.

Spirits typically communicate with me through clairaudience first before I receive any other psychic information from them, which is not always the case for mediums. I find that I can hear spirits pretty well, and often hear them speaking to me very clearly. When a client hears their loved one's name out loud it makes a huge difference, and not only is it about hearing and saying the name but it is often about specific nicknames as well. It creates more validity for the person who receives the readings. These names come into my awareness in the form of a mental mind voice, and even if they sound odd or I'm not 100 percent sure, I say it anyway.

In season two of *Spirit Talker*, I spoke with Ed and his sister Crystal. I was connecting to their mother in Spirit and was partway through the reading when the name Butch came up, which was her nickname for her son Ed. In my mind I thought she was referring to someone else, which serves as a good example to demonstrate that I am receiving these messages outside myself and often don't know who they are in reference to.

When I receive a name and Spirit provides me with information, I am just the middle person. When I hear a name in my mind it typically means that they are telling me who they are, who they are with, and who they are connected to. They can be either living or deceased and sometimes you won't always know right away. It's just how this form of communication works. Sometimes you can tell who's speaking in Spirit, but oftentimes you can't. It's about learning to trust what you receive and then relaying the information, because it's really about that validation for the person you are speaking with. Allowing the messages to flow through you leads you to that next piece of the puzzle, which I refer to as those bread crumbs moments that lead you further down the path of psychic connection.

There are simple exercises that can help you develop your clairaudient abilities and can assist in the process of inviting spirits to connect with you that are from the light. This can be done through prayer, intention, and actively inviting spirits to communicate with you. You can offer them smoke from your smudge and invite them into your awareness. I also recommend praying to release any fears you have around connecting to Spirit, to assist in fully becoming more sensitive and receptive to their messages.

One exercise that I suggest is to count to 10 slowly and then add a letter: 1a, 2b, 3c, 4d, 5e, 6f, 7g, 8h, 9i, 10j, etc. You can do this during those moments you set aside for prayer and meditation and allow it to become part of your daily practice. I also recommend randomly thinking of different names in your mind as well, such as Jim, Mary, Joy, and Margaret. This can also be done in alphabetical order or randomly; either way you should allow the names to flow into your awareness and change them up, because when spirits do speak it is soft and subtle and can easily be missed if you are not focused and aware of your thoughts.

Although most of the clairaudient messages I receive come to me in the form of free-flowing thoughts that are inserted into my awareness by a spirit in the light, I will occasionally hear a voice outside myself that I can record on a device that comes from a higher level of energy that is not an earthbound spirit. I have recorded my guide Victoria on multiple occasions. I know that our guides are always with us, and helping us, and they have empathy for the spirits that have not transcended or moved into the light themselves. She helps me with my work and has assisted me with transitioning earthbound spirits into the light. While I was on McNab's Island located within Halifax Harbor, I had an encounter with a spirit by the name of Howard Carter.

I could hear his voice and was able to record him saying his name. What was so powerful about that audio recording is that my guide Victoria could also be heard during that same session. After Howard Carter's voice can be heard speaking his name, Victoria is clearly recorded saying, "The light way, the light is," meaning that the light is the way to go. I know that it was her way of helping him find his way into the light, and that she was working with me to help guide him to make that journey home.

It was one of those profound moments that I reflect upon often: Victoria helped guide that man's spirit into the light, and that light is a very real place. When I speak about the visitation I received from my father after he passed away, and I mention that light, this is what I am referring to. It isn't a figment of my imagination, it's not a religious belief, it's just as real as you or me.

That audio recording serves as a reminder of that divine source light, which sometimes feels like it is outside of ourselves when it's all around us. In the same way my guide can communicate with me and your guides can communicate with you, our loved ones are never far from us, and want us to know that they are loving us from where they are.

As you strengthen your own ability to communicate with the spirit world and learn the universal language of Spirit for yourself, that connection will become stronger. Not only for yourself and your departed loved ones, but also through your ability to bridge those worlds and pierce the veil. As you practice clairaudience let whatever comes through flow into your awareness. If you hear an earth-bound spirit, pray for guidance to assist in transitioning them into the light. Remember that those within the light guide us from a place of love, and only love.

PRACTICE YOUR CLAIRAUDIENCE

Clairaudience can be developed by working with your inner voice and intentionally speaking names, dates, and phrases within your own mind. Put some time aside each day and practice. The more adept you become, the easier this next exercise will be.

Do this exercise with a friend who is open to your development or with a group who is developing their psychic abilities.

When sitting with people, be mindful and present, as a mind full of thoughts and chatter is neither a clear mind nor an open mind for clairaudient impressions.

Say a prayer you have written ("Words Have Power" exercise) and invite your Ancestors, guides, and angels to help you receive a clairaudient impression in relation to guiding someone or connecting to your friends' loved ones through clairaudient impressions.

Engage in the mindful meditation with eyes-open exercise, without holding an image ("Create Space to Receive" chapter). Be present and mindful of what names, words, dates come into your awareness. Most times it will seem as if it just pops into your head out of the blue. It may be a song you hear in your inner audible thoughts.

Trust whatever you receive and ask the person or group if they know anyone by that name. If it is a date, ask why this date is important. If you hear a phrase, ask if someone used to speak this phrase in their circle of friends or family in the spirit world. If it is a song, what song is it? Does the song have meaning to the person you are speaking with?

Work with what is given and try to validate to the best of your ability. This will become more natural once you get into the flow of receiving, trusting, and validating.

CHAPTER 36

PILUE'L KLE'L

THE OTHER "CLAIRS"

As I have discussed in previous chapters, spirits are always communicating with us, and often do so in ways most people don't recognize or even remember. This communication comes through as a universal language everyone has access to; it can be learned. It is a language of energy that can be grasped, interpreted, and even spoken, and once you allow Spirit into your life and express to them your desire to communicate, you will be amazed at how your life begins to unfold.

In previous chapters I have focused on some of the other "Clairs": clairsentience, clairvoyance, and clairaudience. All of which are pivotal for the work that I do and for learning the language of Spirit on a deeper level, but I'm going to touch upon a few of the other "Clairs" that can also be powerful ways to receive Spirit messages as well.

Claircognizance means clear knowing, and usually is conveyed without words or reason. A claircognizant person is somebody who simply knows things about a person, place, object, or even concepts without being told any additional information, which can pertain to the past, present, and even future events. These messages come into the mind, and you just know that the information and wisdom you received is correct.

People with these psychic abilities can be quite logical and tend to receive psychic information through spontaneous ideas. They enjoy figuring out answers for longstanding problems and finding solutions creatively. They often have an answer for everything and understand issues even when they are not well versed in the subject matter or do not even understand where the information came from.

In the final episode of season three of *Spirit Talker* I spoke with Jenna, a woman who had recently realized that she was pregnant with her third child. I instantly knew that she was pregnant, and her grandmom communicated additional messages letting me know that Jenna had some issues with anemia with her past pregnancies. She wanted Jenna to be comforted in knowing that she would get through it all, and she would just need to see beyond her present circumstances and trust that it would all be okay. In this case I trusted the information I received and communicated the message. Typically, telling a woman she's pregnant isn't something I do, but when I receive a message from Spirit, I trust and say it anyway.

Sometimes claircognizance is experienced in the form of suddenly knowing not to do a certain activity, to meet up with a certain person, or to avoid a specific area. There have been cases of people who decided not to board an airplane and then tragically the plane crashed, or when your phone rings and you instantly know who's on the other line. This all falls under claircognizant impressions. Although this form of spirit communication is less common, it can be very enlightening when it does happen. I have claircognizant moments in my own life, which usually appear during one of my favorite pastimes.

I love playing poker with friends and have competed and won a few tournaments throughout my life. I would consider myself to be a skilled poker player and have even freaked out some of my buddies when playing. I believe poker is a great skill to have and one that can even assist in strengthening claircognizant abilities—especially if you practice by tuning in to which cards will be turned over next. Sometimes I just know what the other person has in their hand; without reason or logic, I just know.

Another form of psychic impression is clear smelling, also known as clairalience. It can be surprising when you receive this type of message from Spirit. You might smell your mother's favorite flowers, or a perfume your grandmother wore, and often it can be very specific. During one of my readings, I could smell Chanel No. 5; it turns out that the woman who had passed had been obsessed with the perfume during her life and received it every year for Christmas.

Within my own personal life, I've also experienced this form of "Clair." On the 29th anniversary of my dad's passing, I woke up to the intense smell of cigarettes, as though someone had blown smoke directly into my face. This was not a physical possibility since no one smoked in our home, but I knew my dad was paying a visit that day.

Sometimes when you receive this form of communication it corresponds with other important messages as well. For example, while I was in Glooscap First Nation filming season two of the series, I spoke with a man and could taste and smell peanut butter cookies. I could tell that his grandmom was showing me a plate of cookies, and that she would always make them for him. I wasn't sure what type they were at first, but I could clearly smell and taste peanut butter, which was one of his favorite things. In this case clairalience and clairgustance were working in harmony to solidify the message that came forward, since the senses of smell and taste are so closely linked.

Clairgustance means clear-tasting and occurs when you taste something on a spiritual level without having to physically put the item in your mouth. I've often found a loved one comes through with this message when it's connected to a favorite dessert. They may also communicate a person had a strong connection to or struggled with marijuana, alcohol, or nicotine, via tasting or smelling one of these substances. It all depends on what other forms of communication Spirit is relaying in those moments, and how the language reveals itself to you.

All these forms of communication are a gift from Spirit. I consider myself to be a good translator, and my hope for you is that you become a translator in your own life through your own spirit connections. If you've had similar experiences in your life or wish to further your own psychic development, I wish for you to follow those bread crumbs that are given during a connection.

You may find the language of Spirit speaks to you more strongly in one area over another, and the idea is to seek out what skills are more prominent in your life and then develop those innate abilities further. By learning to trust in the messages that you receive, the rest will follow. If you don't understand the message initially, don't be discouraged—I don't always know either sometimes, even after over 25 years of experience in this field. I'm still learning, and I feel that Spirit is still continuously working with me to grow my vocabulary and intuition, my inner psychic knowledge.

I want to encourage you to trust in the information even when you're unsure, because the meaning may reveal itself to you later. I've learned to trust. I've learned that I may not know all the answers, but what I can do is convey what Spirit would like to communicate. I tell whoever I'm with what comes through because they will undoubtedly understand the message; if they don't immediately, they will eventually figure it out.

Remember to always set your intention to Spirit that the communication you receive be from a good place, and to help heal the hearts of the people you are working with. Before any reading I ask my spirit guides for assistance and let them know that I am open to receive and willing to accept the messages that come to me— however that looks! I completely let go of expectations of how the information should come through and how things will unfold, but I work with what I receive and I am thankful to be part of the process. We are all on our own journeys in this life, and I wish everyone reading these words today will find joy and delight as you further your own psychic abilities and become more fluent in the universal language of Spirit.

With claircognizance, there really is no way to develop other than trusting and blurting out the information you were just infused with about a person, alive or passed, or about a certain situation. It is an infused, direct understanding from the spirit world that comes with knowing, without knowing how you know. The more you trust and work with this ability the more it will flow into your psychic life.

EXERCISE TO DEVELOP AND GROW CLAIRALIENCE AND CLAIRGUSTANCE

Emphasize on tasting and smelling all your food that is pleasant to you.

Another great way to develop your clairgustance and clairalience skills is to develop your palate! Go out into the world and try new things!

Smell all spiritual medicines you use prior to smudging.

Meditate on familiar smells and tastes like tea, coffee, chocolate, perfume, flowers, sea air, cookies, lemons, etc. Really work at this more and more to build a vast vocabulary of these two senses.

CHAPTER 37

K'JIJITAQNN WEJIAQL A'SE'K

WISDOM FROM THE OTHER SIDE

I have visited the other side during my life and have experienced several insights while in this state of existence. I have found so much solace and have immense gratitude for being aware that there is so much more to life than our current realities. I am blessed with having a deep connection to the spirit world and the understanding of what happens to us between our lifetimes.

Two experiences that profoundly impacted how I see the other side took place during dreamtime while I was in a lucid state. In my first encounter I realized quickly that I was in spirit form, and was cognizant of where I was but not entirely sure if I had astral-traveled there or if I was somehow reviewing a memory of a time prior to my present incarnation. In the dream I was attending an event, and we were gathering there in spirit form. We had all congregated to this place to hear one person speak, and there were millions of people eagerly awaiting to hear these words of wisdom. I knew I was about to witness something of immense spiritual value.

Although I can't remember who this person was or the specifics of what was said, I knew it was someone of great importance who was bestowing wisdom upon us. It could have been a great philosopher teaching about the human condition, or a profoundly spiritual person like Jesus speaking about a universal truth. Whatever the case, we were all guided to be present for this monumental occasion.

Whether or not I remember the words that were spoken is less important than what I learned about the other side that day. The truth is my soul remembers, and I carry that wisdom with me, even if I can't access it from my memories alone. I just know that we were all eager to attend this event and hear this important teaching.

When I arrived at the building it was reminiscent of Romanesque architecture, like the historic structure of the Coliseum in Rome, but more imposing. The stadium was immense and dwarfed any building here on Earth, and each of us was dressed in solid white robes, which is always the case during visions I have received and from my interactions with those from the other side. That isn't to say everyone uniformly wears the same thing, but typically most people wear white, and those who don't have chosen their clothing for a specific reason.

We all began to take our seats, and as I did, I transitioned from my physical body to an orb of pure energy and light. I found my spot without any thought or effort, which was three-quarters of the way up, and when I took my place and looked around, I could see millions there in attendance. We were all in spirit form, and we were all there to witness this person's speech.

The interesting thing was even though this person was miles away and standing at the center of the stage, as they spoke, I could still see them clearly. My perception was unlike what it is here on Earth because I could see this person speak as though they were only 50 feet away from me. I was given the impression that no matter where you sat within this structure everyone was given a front-row seat. So it was irrelevant where you were, and regardless of whether you were at the top, the middle, or at the bottom, our perceptions were all the same.

As the person finished speaking, I realized we all needed to be in this energetic form to take up less space so we all could be in attendance. That way we could all be there and take part in this teaching and receive the wisdom without the confines of a physical body. I was thinking about how amazing it was to hear this person speak, and that they could share their words and impart what they had learned from their multitude of lifetimes.

Even though I had returned to my body, as I left the auditorium, and was once again wearing a white robe, I noticed not everyone regained their physical appearance. Some people did, but others remained formless or chose a different form entirely. I felt we had a choice to take on our appearance from other lifetimes, and it wasn't an ego-based decision but based on which visual representation resonated more strongly with us. Perhaps the people who chose a different body felt closer to that lifetime and had achieved all that their soul wanted in that incarnation and was the perfection of what they wanted in terms of soul development. Some chose to remain as orbs and still hadn't moved into form, which was a choice that resonated more strongly with others.

Not that they needed to look like anyone or anything other than the orb, but I took note that some of us chose not to take on a physical form after the speech was over. It seemed like everyone was going off on their own, and I felt I had somewhere I needed to be and began moving in the direction I was meant to go.

I could feel on a clairsentient level that my soul family, my soul tribe, was all there with me. All my guides, friends, and family, and all those who I have loved through my many incarnations were all present. Even people from other lives were there, some of whom I feel even closer to than I do in this lifetime. It was through a soul recognition that certain people there felt more familiar than others, and I could feel a type of kindred spirit connection between us that transcended not only this realm, but I knew we had experienced many lifetimes together.

There were entertainers, performers, and great speakers who shared their wisdom with the masses, and in many ways our physical reality pales in comparison. The other side is indescribable, and sometimes worldly terms just don't seem to measure up when trying to express the beauty of it all. Everything on Earth just seemed smaller and less pronounced, but there are still familiar places, like forests, mountains, and oceans. It just feels a bit muted in comparison.

As I left and continued toward my unknown destination, I took in my surroundings. I noticed how much brighter everything was and how light seemed to permeate all things, and how all my senses seemed more enhanced. I observed the trees and could hear the birds and watched as they flew past me. I smelled how clean and fresh the air was, and I looked out over the water and could see many animals living peacefully.

They were going about their own lives in harmony, which is something I've been aware of through my mediumship work, but it was still nice to see animals living happily on the other side. I took in the incredible sky that was different from our own, and the sun had a reddish hue. It felt more vivid than in real life and like a heightened state of reality that was much more expansive.

Wherever I thought I should be I could just go toward; I didn't have to walk there. My feeling is that, while I was in this form, wherever my awareness went, I would just go to that place. Everyplace and anyone that I wanted to visit was just a thought away and required zero effort.

I took this dream of sorts to mean what I know is true: we will all make our journey to this place at the end of our earthly lives, and it is an incredible aspect of life that is meant to be looked forward to rather than something we fear. On the other side there is a place we all visit, which is individual to each of us. Some of us will meet in a valley, or by the ocean, or some other special place, and it's where we will reunite with those people we love.

The purpose for us to live our lives on Earth and to experience challenges is ultimately for our continued growth and evolution. The greatest gift we are given is the ability to leave that place and come here and live our lives so that we can be taught lessons that we can't learn there. So we can develop, and struggle, and become more enlightened individuals because of it all. It may not always seem like a gift, but our lives are transient, and so is the pain we experience here. You may lose your life, or lose your way, but the truth is you will always come back again. It's a never-ending continuation of the evolution of our soul that will go on forever in this world, and I'm certain will continue in other worlds after that.

In between our many lifetimes and before we incarnate into the physical world we learn and prepare for the lives we will live here on Earth, and during this incredibly vivid and lucid dream I saw universities and great halls of wisdom. Our life themes are chosen for a reason, and with a higher purpose in mind, and special care and preparation takes place for us to fully understand what we will experience during our lifetimes. We study from the akashic records in the great hall and choose our guides based on individuals who have had similar life themes and have a good understanding of the challenges we will face. The truth is we are never alone, and we can't come into this life alone—no one ever does.

I remember another dream that took place in which I attended one of these university classes and was once again wearing a white robe. I was with someone and couldn't make out who they were, but I felt they were one of my spirit guides, most likely Sam. We were in a classroom where a professor was giving a lecture, and a man stood in front of the class and was speaking about our life charts, and how all aspects of our lives are coded within our DNA in a secret language we have yet to discover.

Aspects of our genetic makeup are encoded into our DNA, such as eye color, hair color, etc. However, in this dream, I was taught that even on a molecular level our DNA already has aspects of our lived experiences programmed within it, such as our life themes, our struggles, and our purpose for being here—everything we will face in this life is already held within us and is written in that same encoded language; we just aren't aware of it yet on a scientific level.

Who we were meant to be in this life, the ways in which we grow as individuals, and how we learn our lessons, was all charted long before we ever opened our eyes and gazed upon the world around us. This isn't a way of discrediting free will—we still have choices and can choose not to pursue what might be charted for us, but I was taught in this dream that the notion of "junk DNA" contains within it our potential futures that have yet to come into existence. In a sense, they are realities we have the choice to unlock within ourselves, but it is still a choice. We might have overarching life themes that were already decided upon, but before this incarnation there were aspects of our life charts left blank that would be chosen as we journeyed through life.

As the dream progressed, the professor took us away from the auditorium, and we were suddenly in a rock quarry. He reached down and touched a blade of grass that was peeking up through the rocks. I questioned the meaning of it all, but as I touched the strand, I was given a sense of its entire life story. I was given information about how this plant came to be, and even in a sense the life of its parents, and the life lessons it was learning by existing in a less than habitable environment.

Suddenly we were back in the classroom and there was a projection of the life chart of this specific plant on the screen. To know that it had its own unique purpose, and that it had a life mapped out before it came into being, was honestly mind boggling for me. We often think in terms of the universe being incomprehensible because of the vastness of space, but what we fail to realize is that even on a small scale, through the example of a small blade of grass, all aspects of our world are equally immeasurable. We tend to focus so much on stars that died long ago that still twinkle in the night sky, and the potential of the hundreds of billions of galaxies that exist in the universe but fail to recognize that it is equally significant to look at the complexity of Mother Earth herself.

I learned an important lesson through that interaction, which I hope to impart to everyone who reads this book. That something so small and seemingly insignificant had a purpose for being here and my human ego hadn't realized that possibility before that encounter. I think as human beings we might assume it's only about us, and that our lives are the only ones that matter, but the reality is it's about everything.

The term Msit No'kmaq means "all my relations" in Mi'kmaq and relates back to this concept and represents our connection to all things and all nations. It speaks to the complex and balanced interaction that exists among the human, plant, spirit, mineral, and animal nations, and how important it is to honor and respect the interconnectedness of all aspects of life.

There is a purpose and plan for the plants, animals, oceans, and everything that calls this world home. They, too, have auras and a spirit and are growing and evolving in their own unique and divine ways. Everything that exists here had to first exist on the other side. This includes technological advancements and even forms of creative expression. There are concepts that were meant to be expressed into this world, and there is an infusion of information that takes place to bring those thoughts, expressions, and ideas into being. That information has always been there, and my belief is that if it didn't exist there first, it wouldn't exist in our physical reality.

Everything within the universe has its own frequency, and I feel that the Creator's intention is for everyone and all things to be able to vibrate at their own divine frequency. If we think of it on a personal level, it might be helpful to imagine the optimal version of yourself, and how that might feel and look. What dreams do you have for yourself, and what areas of your life do you wish to improve? I think each of us individually can make self-improvements, and by becoming the best versions of ourselves, living a peaceful existence would help each of us find our way back to that divine frequency that the Creator intended us to return to. If we can make that version of ourselves a solid reality, we could create a new and better world for everyone.

We are all a sacred piece of the Creator and possess a unique aspect of the Divine. I believe we all have the potential to shift and change our own realities. By adjusting our thoughts, initiating those actions, and taking the necessary steps, we can bring those potential realities into the physical world.

I think we can often become overwhelmed by the challenges of this world and the harshness of it all, but it isn't necessary to focus on the grand scale and expect to change all the negative aspects of life. Begin with yourself and find what brings you joy, and work from there. The universe expresses itself through each one of us, and it's about looking inward and focusing on your own journey. Living life in a gentle way, and by remembering that we are all relations and we are all one, we can embody those unconditionally loving aspects that I have witnessed on the other side.

Remember to honor the spirit in everything that you experience. As an Indigenous person I am taught to respect all things, as they have a purpose for being here. I was taught to never take anything without giving something in return. I am grateful for the oceans, rocks, trees, flowers, animals, and even my grass growing outside my home. I am taught if I take something that I offer something in return like Tobacco, which is a sacred medicine to Indigenous people. It's a medicine that I place my prayer of gratitude and thanks intentionally into. I leave that Tobacco offering in return, if I take something to use in my life.

You may not be Indigenous in the sense of culture in common speaking terms, but we are all Indigenous to the spirit and physical worlds! Be mindful and respect all things, Spirit and physical. Speak your own prayers of gratitude and unconditional love for all things, and remember we are all one. Make that your offering and leave it wherever you may go.

PRAYER TO ENTER THE SPIRIT WORLD AND LEARN IN YOUR DREAMTIME

Great Spirit, Creator, spirit guides, and Ancestors, hear my prayer.

I ask you take me to the great temples and halls of wisdom and knowledge in the spirit world.

Help me remember and learn within my dreamtime about our oneness and interconnectedness.

I am available to align with my higher purpose.

I can and will be a messenger for truth and knowledge here in the physical world.

In return I will share with all who will listen.

Thank you, all my relations for hearing my words and prayer.

Wela'lin, Msit No'kmaq

CHAPTER 38

NEWKEWE'L JIPUKTEWE'L KINA'MAQNN

THE FOUR SACRED FIRE TEACHINGS

Part of the process of filming my TV series involves learning more about the diverse Indigenous cultures that can be found within Canada. I offer healing messages and speak with Elders in each community I visit, and they in turn offer me traditional wisdom that I can share with others through the medium of television.

The first two seasons of the series were filmed in Atlantic Canada and gave me the opportunity to connect more with Mi'kmaq and Maliseet communities, while also deepening my own understanding of some of my family's roots and traditions. We filmed the third season in Ontario and Quebec, where I was able to meet with several different Mohawk and Ojibwa community members. During this time I met with Patricia Toulouse, who comes from a long line of medicine women and who herself is a traditional Ojibwa medicine woman.

We traveled to the largest lake island in the world, Manitoulin Island, which is found within Lake Huron, and while we were out looking for fossils, I mentioned to her that I was planning to attend a sacred fire ceremony. Although I have been to many sacred fires in my life, I had never received teachings from a fire keeper specifically about their important role within the community.

Patricia then taught me about the four Sacred Fire teachings, which I had not yet come across. She explained to me that fire is sacred to all of creation, and it is recognized as a living thing. In the same way respect should be given to the human nation or to the animal nation, respect should also be given to the different forms of Sacred Fire.

The first Sacred Fire is our sun, which radiates its rays upon us, and the warmth and light it emanates make it possible for life to exist here on Earth. We circle the sun, thanks to its gravity, and it rests in the center of the solar system, and this energetic force provides us with the necessities for life. It also creates the seasons we experience here on our planet, which also relates to the four sacred seasons of our lives: infancy, youth, adulthood, and Elder—since there is a season for everything and a sacredness to each phase we go through in our journey in life.

The sun reminds us of the Creator, and that we are part of that sacred light, and everyone is made from the minerals of long-forgotten stars. We are all stardust, and we are literally made from that same material that makes up the countless number of suns in the universe. So when we look at the stars in the night sky or feel the warmth of our Grandfather Sun, we are reminded of that Sacred Fire. When we remember to give thanks for that divine light it is also important to know that the Creator's vision for our world included you and me, and everyone we know. It all started with that first light—the Sacred Fire of the Grandfather Sun.

Patricia continued, explaining that the Sacred Fire is found in the center of our world. It is the fire contained within the core of Mother Earth, and was formed from the same stardust that created us and our Grandfather Sun. The magma—the heat contained within the core—represents the light that shines and emanates out into the world. It creates the gravity that holds us to the earth itself, our atmosphere, the rock formations, and all the amazing events that have taken place within our own lives.

That core blood that flows within her created all that we see here today and is responsible for the totality of all human experience. Every moment that has ever happened in the history of our world was a result of this coming into existence.

The third Sacred Fire is our ceremonial fire, because within Indigenous culture we are taught that the Sacred Fire of the sun is the light of creation itself. This energy, this force, is not only part of our solar system, and contained inside the core of Mother Earth, it is also held within the flames of our ceremonial fires.

This Sacred Fire is used in all our ceremonies and is the fire we create outside of ourselves and is the one we send out into the world. It serves as a spiritual doorway to the spirit realm, so that when someone dies, or during celebrations such as a pipe ceremony or sweat lodge, we light a sacred fire to honor those who have come before us. This way we can communicate with our relations who have been with us from the beginning and until the end of time.

The fire continually burns, and it is an immense responsibility to be a fire keeper, because their job is to protect and feed the fire during those four days. The fire keeper ensures that the kindling is good, and the fuel that you feed the fire is the best wood. You wouldn't use wet or soggy pieces but only ones that would burn well, and this is also true for the prayers you offer to the fire itself.

When you say your prayers, you should come from a pure-hearted, and positive place. As you speak your intentions and hold the Tobacco over your heart and give that bundle to the fire as an offering to the Creator, your prayers rise into the air. This allows for your intentions to be carried along with the smoke of the Sacred Fire, and for the words you speak to rise into the ether that surrounds us all and reach up into the heavens where the eagles soar, so to speak.

This form of sacred fire reminds us of our connection to the first light of the Grandfather Sun, and to our connection to the fire contained within the heart of Mother Earth. It is also a teaching tool for us about the importance of ensuring that not only do we tend to our ceremonial fires in a good and positive way, but it also serves as a reminder of the need to look after and care for ourselves, through the purity of our words and thoughts, and to feel good emotions that fuel the passion within the center of our being.

This leads us to the fourth Sacred Fire, which is the heart's Sacred Fire, and it is the flame found inside everyone. It is the fire that burns within each of our hearts and is the sacred light that was placed inside each person by the Creator. It is just as sacred as any ceremonial fire that we create in the physical world. We tend to the sacred fire within ourselves by moving through life in a good way and by treating ourselves and others with kindness and respect. We can release and let go of "bad kindling" or "bad medicine" so that we can be more aligned with our higher purpose. So, as we energize our spiritual selves with the only fuel it truly needs, unconditional love, we are reminded that this is the same love that exists inside our Grandfather Sun. This is the same fire that exists within the core of Mother Earth and is ignited by our sacred fires, which burn within each of our hearts.

As we honor the Four Sacred Fire Teachings, we learn that we are all connected in this one great and beautiful creation of life. Each one of us has a purpose for being here, and everything is in alignment for us to have and experience what we were meant to express into this world. Without the sun, without the core, and without our ceremonies and prayers, we would not be heard. It is by holding unconditional love in our hearts and by being nonjudgmental to ourselves, and to others, that we learn to be in balance with that sacred light found within the Four Sacred Fire Teachings.

I thanked Patricia for the knowledge she gave to me, which I will carry throughout my journey in life. I continued my travels to another community on Manitoulin Island called M'Chigeeng. This area is part of the council of the Three Fires, which is a long-standing alliance between the Ojibwe, Odawa, and Potawatomi tribes. I was greeted there by some community members, who prepared a sacred ceremonial fire with me.

I spoke with Elder Alma Jean, Josh, and fire keeper apprentice Blaine and explained to them the teachings that I had received from Patricia the day before. Although I was very much learning from them that day, I was happy and honored to share what I learned about the Four Sacred Fires.

A big part of my culture is teaching by sharing knowledge with others, and that day served as an example of this value. I believe we were able to impart knowledge to one another, and in doing so those Four Sacred Fire Teachings became part of their wisdom, too. These teachings had gone from one person to another to another and could now enrich the experience of the Fire Keepers and their own personal connection to the Four Sacred Fires.

One aspect of that day I found interesting was that at the age of 32, Blaine is still considered an apprentice, even after 20 years of experience. The role of a fire keeper is an immense responsibility, and despite his many years gaining knowledge and wisdom he is still considered an apprentice. He spoke about having a small bundle, and that the sacred items he receives are given to him through the passage of time. He earns his gifts through the spiritual work that he does, and his community is passing him the torch to become the lead fire keeper.

I think there is good wisdom to be shared after speaking with Blaine about the lessons we learn in life, and the wisdom we gain because of them. Our journey is a sacred one, and we won't know all the answers immediately. The reason Elders in my culture are so revered and appreciated is because my ancestors placed importance on gaining wisdom through time, and through life experiences.

Many of us can go off track, or forget who we are and why we are even here, but it is important to remember that our path in life is a unique one that should be celebrated rather than compared to the journeys experienced by others. We all have a distinct set of life circumstances that we experience during our time here. We learn from and teach others throughout our lives in the physical world. We are all students and teachers and are all pieces to some divine puzzle.

On an individual level, we all represent a different spark of the Divine, and in the same way there are no two snowflakes that are the same. The light that shines within our heart is unique to ourselves and is a connection to the Creator. Through the process of honoring our path, no matter how different it may look to others, and by being in alignment with our higher purpose, we honor ourselves; it is by respecting the desires we have for our life that we honor the Four Sacred Fires.

The same sacred light that burns within each of our hearts allows us to be connected to the ceremonial fires we ignite during our ceremonies, and to the intentions and prayers that are carried up into the spirit world and to the Creator. It allows us to feel grounded to the energy within Mother Earth and the Sacred Fire of her core, so that we can marvel at the wonders found on our planet and the vast array of experiences that have resulted because of her existence.

This serves as a reminder of our divine and unique connection to the Creator through our relationship to Grandfather Sun. We were all meant to experience life and have an impact on the lives of others. We are meant to remind the people we encounter of their own divinity and in doing so can make their journey through life a little easier. We help any weight they carry along with them become less burdensome. This doesn't mean that we all need to become spirit talkers, or speak on a stage, or spread a message through a TV show, but rather it is about finding your own unique voice and using it to help others in the process.

This is part of the reason why I love filming *Spirit Talker* so much: I can learn these teachings from Elders and then share their wisdom to a wider audience. There is no greater gift in life than to be able to assist others in their lives, and by utilizing Indigenous teachings. My hope is that more understanding will be shared across all cultures, since these teachings were never meant to be stored away but are connected to universal wisdom that was meant to be shared with everyone. We are all Indigenous to this world!

KESPIAQ

CONCLUSION

Spiritual work is required to raise your energetic vibration. You will be amazed at how much your life can change for the better when you begin a practice of prayerful words, meditation, focusing on your chakras, and by being mindful of how you move through life. By intentionally coming from an unconditionally loving place, you will see profound changes not only for yourself, but you will also begin to realize how much impact you can have to effectively change how others see and interact with the world around them.

We must all move to a higher level of consciousness, and to a more spiritually focused place, because what we are currently doing isn't working and hasn't been for some time. By becoming more connected, more psychic, more attuned with each other, focusing on empathy and coming from a place of understanding, the better our world will be. The more you see the light in others and allow others to see that same light within themselves, the brighter we all shine together. It will begin to radiate outward from within you and will begin to permeate all facets of life, and remove any shred of doubt or darkness.

I've touched on the expression of Msit No'kmaq, or "all my relations," throughout this book and feel it's about the unconditional connection between us all. All my relations is about balance, that we can choose to strengthen our connection to one another and make it more expansive; that we seek to rise above our old selves, and beliefs, and find a better way forward; so that we can, in effect, walk on water together.

As you begin to open yourself up to the possibility of it all, you will change and deepen in ways people won't understand or believe. There might be some reluctance on their part because they're not there yet and can't see life the way you do. By removing limiting beliefs from your vocabulary, and by knowing that so much is possible, you can be prepared to witness miracles in your own life

By changing your thoughts and your words, you can shift your life and be able to reach a higher level of connection that you wouldn't have dreamed possible. By growing spiritually, you will begin to see changes all around you. It's through developing your intuition and serving the Creator in the best way you can so that the positive internal light that you exude will ripple out into the world and affect your environment. It's a conscious choice you can make, and one that can have a great impact for those willing to shift how they view and approach the spirit world.

The point isn't to solely offer insight on how to be a spirit talker or psychic medium, but rather about living life from an unconditional loving perspective, being mindful of what thoughts and intentions you're putting out into the world, and by being fully present.

You might be guided to actively begin your own journey to becoming a professional psychic medium, but that is an individual journey that only you will know the answer to. Not everyone will be guided in that direction, but healing is necessary for the inhabitants of Mother Earth. Helping heal the hearts and souls that you encounter is a gift of living a more spiritually elevated life.

When you walk above the negativity you face and the hardships of the world, you will notice an inner resolve that was once absent. You will be tested, but in those moments lean on your spirit team to help get you through it all and hold on to the memory of your loved ones. Your Ancestors, angels, guides, and the Creator are always with you and have always been there.

Within Indigenous Culture we begin each of our ceremonies facing the eastern direction. The dawn's first light is felt along the horizon and begins to flood outward, touching everything as the sun begins to rise. That light is a reminder of the Creator and the unconditional love that shines upon all of us, and there is no one on this Earth that the sun shines on more than another.

That love is there for all of us, even for those who have made major mistakes in this life. That loving light shines on every nation equally: every plant, animal, mineral, spirit, and human nation is surrounded by a stronger force than we can comprehend, one that loves every one of us equally. So, if you are able to go outside, then I suggest greeting that early light and feeling that warmth upon you, and remember that love and divine connection is available to all of us.

As you remember to honor Mother Earth and all of her inhabitants through a gentle approach to the land, the rivers, the oceans, the animals, the people of every faith and culture, and most importantly by honoring yourself, you will see major changes. By approaching all things with love, you will begin to radiate an energy that others will aspire to, and by helping others be a guiding light in the darkness, you can someday help others learn to walk on water, too.

Wela'lin, thank you.

Mist No'kmaq. All my relations.

ACKNOWLEDGMENTS

I want to thank my ghostwriter, Danielle MacQuarrie, for helping put my thoughts and experiences onto the page. Gratitude to John Holland for touring with me and introducing Hay House to who I am and what I do.

I thank my literary agent Michele Martin and editor Anna Cooperberg, who did an amazing job as my editor. Thank you to Patricia Gift, the vice president and publisher at Hay House, for believing in me and my work, and Reid Tracy, president at Hay House, for encouraging writers who help inspire the world.

A special thank you to Anne Marie Marchand for providing Mi'kmaq translations.

Thank you to Dr. Wayne W. Dyer, whose words inspired me in my life, and who continues to inspire me in the spirit world.

I thank all my students in Spirit Talker Tribe who continue my legacy of helping heal the hearts of others, which makes me immensely proud.

Lastly, I want to thank Michelle Beaupre, my beautiful wife, for supporting me as my partner in this life.

Wela'lin, thank you.

ABOUT THE AUTHOR

Shawn Leonard is a heart-centered Mi'kmaq psychic medium and the star and host of APTN TV's show *Spirit Talker*. Taking an authentic approach to the spirit world in his readings, live shows, and media appearances, Shawn imparts enormous wisdom and knowledge of the spirit world and spirit communication. He teaches the Spirit Talker Tribe online course to hundreds of students every year.

Hay House Titles of Related Interest

YOU CAN HEAL YOUR LIFE, the movie,
starring Louise Hay & Friends
(available as an online streaming video)
www.hayhouse.com/louise-movie

THE SHIFT, the movie,
starring Dr. Wayne W. Dyer
(available as an online streaming video)
www.hayhouse.com/the-shift-movie

***

YOU ARE THE MEDICINE: 13 Moons of Indigenous Wisdom, Ancestral Connection, and Animal Spirit Guidance by Asha Frost

THINK INDIGENOUS: Native American Spirituality for a Modern World by Doug Good Feather

WOMAN BETWEEN THE WORLDS: A Call to Your Ancestral and Indigenous Wisdom by Apela Colorado

KINDLING THE NATIVE SPIRIT: Sacred Practices for Everyday Life by Denise Linn

All of the above are available at your local bookstore,
or may be ordered by contacting Hay House (see next page).

***

We hope you enjoyed this Hay House book. If you'd like to receive our online catalog featuring additional information on Hay House books and products, or if you'd like to find out more about the Hay Foundation, please contact:

Hay House, Inc., P.O. Box 5100, Carlsbad, CA 92018-5100
(760) 431-7695 or (800) 654-5126
(760) 431-6948 (fax) or (800) 650-5115 (fax)
www.hayhouse.com® • www.hayfoundation.org

———

Published in Australia by: Hay House Australia Pty. Ltd.,
18/36 Ralph St., Alexandria NSW 2015
Phone: 612-9669-4299 • *Fax:* 612-9669-4144
www.hayhouse.com.au

Published in the United Kingdom by: Hay House UK, Ltd.,
The Sixth Floor, Watson House, 54 Baker Street, London W1U 7BU
Phone: +44 (0)20 3927 7290 • *Fax:* +44 (0)20 3927 7291
www.hayhouse.co.uk

Published in India by: Hay House Publishers India,
Muskaan Complex, Plot No. 3, B-2, Vasant Kunj, New Delhi 110 070
Phone: 91-11-4176-1620 • *Fax:* 91-11-4176-1630
www.hayhouse.co.in

———

<u>Access New Knowledge.</u>
<u>Anytime. Anywhere.</u>

Learn and evolve at your own pace
with the world's leading experts.

www.hayhouseU.com